MW01101983

Conrad's Sensational Heroines

Ellen Burton Harrington

Conrad's Sensational Heroines

Gender and Representation in the Late Fiction
of Joseph Conrad

Ellen Burton Harrington
Department of English
University of South Alabama
Mobile, AL, USA

ISBN 978-3-319-63296-4   ISBN 978-3-319-63297-1   (eBook)
DOI 10.1007/978-3-319-63297-1

Library of Congress Control Number: 2017948261

Cover illustration taken from *The female offender* (1895) by Cesare Lombroso, Guglielmo
Ferrero, and William Douglas Morrison

Printed on acid-free paper

This Palgrave Macmillan imprint is published by Springer Nature
The registered company is Springer International Publishing AG
The registered company address is: Gewerbestrasse 11, 6330 Cham, Switzerland

ACKNOWLEDGEMENTS

I am grateful to those generous colleagues and dear friends at the University of South Alabama who read drafts and talked through possibilities—John Halbrooks, Susan McCready, Chris Raczkowski, and Steve Trout. The support of the English Department and the College of Arts and Sciences enabled me to travel to present papers and confer with colleagues, and the university's Arts and Humanities grant program funded the indexing of the book. I appreciate the enthusiastic research assistance of Frank Ard several years ago when he was a graduate student and I was just beginning this project, as well as the tireless work of Debbie Cobb and the staff at the Marx Library to secure distant volumes to augment our local collection. I am fortunate to have many other colleagues at the university who have offered their encouragement and advice over the years, including Kristina Busse, Richard Hillyer, Cris Hollingsworth, and Justin St. Clair.

My sincere thanks to my mentor at Tulane, Geoffrey Galt Harpham, for introducing me to Conrad when he was working on *One of Us* all those years ago. The Conrad community has been a warm and welcoming one, and I very much appreciate the interest and support of my fellow scholars since my student days. Debra Romanick Baldwin and Jack Peters have shared their work with me and encouraged my work in Conrad studies over the years. Thanks to Joyce Wexler for sharing the unpublished manuscript of her essay on *The Rescue* with me as I drafted the sixth chapter.

Allie Bochicchio and Emily Janakiram, as well as Ryan Jenkins, at Palgrave have been particularly helpful, and the anonymous reviewer provided thoughtful constructive advice that helped refine the project.

Earlier versions of two chapters were published in *Conradiana* and *The Conradian*: "'Dead men have no children' in Conrad's 'The Idiots' and 'Amy Foster.'" *Conradiana:* 43 (2–3) in 2011 and "Suicide, Feminism, and 'the miserable dependence of girls' in 'The Idiots,' *The Secret Agent*, and *Chance*." *The Conradian* 37 (2) in 2012. I am grateful to be able to incorporate them here.

My heartfelt thanks go to my parents and my sister for their encouragement; to my children, Patrick and Anna, for their joy in the idea of this book and the distractions they frequently provided from it; and to Dan for his unfailing goodwill, support, and care.

CONTENTS

ABBREVIATIONS

The following abbreviations have been used for Conrad's published works. Unless indicated otherwise, quotations are from the widely available Doubleday, Page, and Company editions published in the early 1920s (New York: Doubleday, Page, and Company, 1920–1925).

AG	*The Arrow of Gold*
C	*Chance*
HD	*Heart of Darkness*
Res	*The Rescue*
Rov	*The Rover*
SA	*The Secret Agent*
SL	*The Shadow-Line*
TLS	*Twixt Land and Sea*
TU	*Tales of Unrest*
TOS	*Typhoon and Other Stories*
V	*Victory*
WT	*Within the Tides*

CHAPTER 1

Introduction: Conrad's Sensational Women

For the reader unfamiliar with the range of Joseph Conrad's work, the author's late fiction makes a surprising turn: the familiar writer of sea stories centered on men moves to consider repeatedly the plight of women and the challenges of renegotiating gender roles in the context of the early twentieth century. Conrad's rich and conflicted consideration of subjectivity and alienation extends to some of his women characters, and his complex use of genre allows him both to prompt and to subvert readers' expectations of popular forms, which typically offer recognizable formulas for gender roles. "But Conrad's best works are never well-wrought," Daphna Erdinast-Vulcan comments in *The Strange Short Fiction of Joseph Conrad* (1999): "It is, in fact, their very defiance of the aesthetics of closure, solidity of structure and generic containment—their 'strangeness', as it were—which makes them so powerful and compelling" (2). This sort of "defiance" on the level of form, a refusal of the aesthetics of nineteenth-century literature and of its generic expectations particularly illuminates Conrad's late work, even when it is not considered his "best" work.

Conrad's fiction draws on multiple genres, including popular fiction, anthropology, and Darwinian science, to respond to Victorian representations of gender in layered and contradictory representations of his own. He uses this generic hybridity to treat gender and femininity in complicated and sometimes conflicting ways. This study seeks to demonstrate how Conrad uses Victorian gender tropes to expose the ways that characters' attitudes about gender and sexuality are shaped by pervasive

© The Author(s) 2017   1
E.B. Harrington, *Conrad's Sensational Heroines*,
DOI 10.1007/978-3-319-63297-1_1

familiar representations, representations that his fiction both takes part in and appraises. By self-consciously alluding to formulaic figures and taxonomies and by portraying representation as a cultural as well as an authorial act, Conrad's late fiction highlights the textual consequences of his aesthetic choices and facilitates a nuanced and contradictory critique of Victorian and *fin-de-siècle* assumptions about women and femininity. Though this study does not address Conrad's political views, Conrad's poetics has political implications as he considers the negative effects of these generic representations, critiquing circumscribed Victorian gender roles framed primarily through the European women characters that are central to a critique of patriarchy as it is practiced in Britain and in the West more generally. His uncompromising and often ironic treatment of representations of women demonstrates their artificiality and the absurdity of the gender hierarchies that underlay such generic figures and taxonomies. Conrad's late fiction displays a willingness to experiment with genre, to inhabit familiar forms and recall sensational figures only to disrupt the preconceptions about gender and genre that his own representations evoke.

It hardly seems controversial to argue that a writer celebrated for his complex treatment of male subjectivity might devote some part of his oeuvre to considering the status of women and the subtleties of men's perceptions and preconceptions about women, yet this perspective requires a shift in the way critics view Conrad in terms of his authorial positioning and his place in modernism. While Conrad addresses gender and subjectivity throughout his work, his later fiction markedly emphasizes women's situations and experiences and men's perspectives on women. Resonant female characters—Susan Bacadou, Winnie Verloc, Flora de Barral, Lena, Alice Jacobus, Rita de Lastaola, and Arlette, among others—are central to Conrad's later works. In these portrayals, he demonstrates a humane sensitivity to his characters' struggles for self-determination in situations that limit their autonomy. Conrad alludes to popular renderings of women's roles in part to consider and critique the expectations of women they create, particularly the issue of women's sexuality, without advocating or envisioning women's liberation within these conventional frames.

In crafting these characters, Conrad responds to a range of representations of women culled from contemporary literature and culture, including the Victorian sensation novel, criminal anthropology, Darwinian science, sentimental fiction, and romance. By evoking pornography and repeatedly describing women displayed for admiration or consumption, Conrad draws attention to representations of women that are objectifying or dehumanizing, displaying a nuanced and perhaps unexpected criticism of Victorian patriarchal conventions. He frames his critique through familiar sensationalized typologies of women demonstrated in his fiction: women as objects of desire, the mother, the murderess, the female suicide, the fallen woman, the adulteress, and the traumatic victim. Considering these figures through the roles and taxonomies that they simultaneously embody and disrupt, this study exposes internalized patriarchal expectations that Conrad presents as both illegitimate and inescapable in his fiction.

In the young captain's alternately sympathetic and objectifying views of Alice in "A Smile of Fortune" (1910), in Heyst's struggle with his fears that Lena's very femininity makes her mercenary towards him in *Victory* (1915), and in George's inability to accept or even comprehend Rita's clear and repeated objections to the way he treats her in *The Arrow of Gold* (1919), Conrad uses men's illusions about women and themselves to critique the nineteenth-century patriarchal structures in literature and culture that such illusions demonstrate. Throughout his late fiction, Conrad portrays characters struggling with the limitations of traditional gender constructions, which he shows to be confining and problematic. Such critiques are made with the characteristic "strangeness" that Erdinast-Vulcan (1999) identifies above, that rejection of closure and "generic containment" that allows Conrad to adapt and complicate the figures and genres to which he refers (2). Thus, melodrama and the other attributes of sensational and popular fiction are invoked only to be ironically undercut, the familiar portrayals exposed as superficial and contradictory—and made strange—in banal drawing rooms, cabins, and hotel lounges the world over.

Critical views on Conrad's relationship to women's fiction have often been damning: for much of the twentieth century, many critics espoused versions of the "achievement and decline" model of Conrad's work, which associates a perceived aesthetic decline in Conrad's late work with Conrad's increased use of the romance genre and his emphasis on female characters. Thomas Moser (1966) codifies this perspective, seeing Conrad's late novels as indicative of his creative "exhaustion" (180); however, such a model fails to note Conrad's continued development and experimentation. As Robert Hampson (1996) explains, "The late novels were not an exhausted return to older subjects as Moser argued, but a continuing experimentation with the novel form for subjects that continued to engage him, and, it must be added, for new subjects as well," particularly women and sexuality (140). In her landmark 1999 study *Conrad and Women*, Susan Jones works to challenge the "achievement and decline" paradigm's "tenacious hold on the critical tradition" by revisiting the assumptions about Conrad's relationship to women in his work and in his literary life to find an "astute, though largely unrecognized, exploration of female identity" in his work (5, 2).[1] Jones responds not just to concerns about Conrad's decline and the valuation of some of his later work, but also to influential feminist critiques, like Nina Pelikan Straus's (1987) powerful reading of Conrad in *Heart of Darkness* (1899) as reinforcing an exclusionary, patriarchal paradigm that is uncongenial to female readers as well as female characters. Considering Conrad's personal and literary relationships with women and some of his late works, Jones demonstrates that Conrad's work engages representations of women to criticize the "patriarchal structures" it reveals with regard to European women (171).

Following Jones, my work offers a more sustained exploration of Conrad's portrayals of women in several of the later novels and a few stories that anticipate them to demonstrate Conrad's preoccupations with women's generic roles and sustained critique of the patriarchal confinement of women. Conrad's fiction repeatedly exposes the fallacy of Victorian patriarchal ideals, like the pretense of benevolent paternalism, which undergirds so much of the cruelty and misbehavior we witness in gender, class, and racial hierarchies in his work: "Conrad's fiction itself exposes the connivance and hypocrisy of male dominance, and, with corrosive cynicism, debunks the claims of a patriarchy which results in the marital servitude of wives" (Simmons 2000, 110). By approaching his critique from within these structures, as it were, Conrad uses juxtaposition and irony to build a scathing vision of the self-interested desire that underlies the pretense of benevolence and the reality of subjugation.

"The time has come to counter the myth of Conrad's misogyny," Carola Kaplan (2005) asserts, demonstrating that even Conrad's early

---

[1] Moser's view is challenged by a range of critics, including ones pertinent to this study like Ruth Nadelhaft in her feminist monograph *Joseph Conrad* (1991), Robert Hampson in *Joseph Conrad: Betrayal and Identity* (1992), and recently Katherine Isobel Baxter's *Joseph Conrad and the Swan Song of Romance* (2010). Indeed, recent scholarship focused on Conrad's late work must always contend to some extent with this presumption of decline.

fictions, including "Karain" (1897) *Heart of Darkness*, and *Lord Jim* (1900), "subvert while appearing to reinforce these patriarchal literary traditions" familiar from significant works of modernism, including homosocial paradigms and the pretense that women are weak and ineffectual (267–269). In Conrad's later works, in particular *Under Western Eyes* (1911), Kaplan argues that Conrad creates not only strong female characters, but women characters whose gender and sexuality are more fluid. Like Kaplan, other recent studies call into question the presumption that gender categories are necessarily polarized and dichotomous in Conrad. In *Conrad's Narratives of Difference: Not Exactly Tales for Boys*, Lissa Schneider (2003) uses a range of approaches to consider the ways that Conrad subverts the masculine aspects of his tales by alluding to feminine genres and imagery in "elusive" ways to create hybrid forms and challenge Victorian cultural norms (3–4). More recently, Debra Romanick Baldwin (2015) shows how Conrad undermines traditional notions of gender, noting of Winnie Verloc in *The Secret Agent* (1907), "the narrative's shifting, anarchic use of gender also forces us to face an *individual*, [...] to confront a passion whose depth and complexity is conveyed not by conventional categories and authoritative voices, but by their explosion" (138). Baldwin considers how Conradian *eros* moves beyond gender in its longing for understanding and intimacy. If some critics propounded views of Conrad's best work as underpinned by a defined and discrete shipboard masculinity complemented by subordinated, objectified female figures, recent criticism instead offers a complex view of gender identity in women on par with Conrad's treatment of other aspects of identity in his work. The present study builds on these works to consider Conrad's strategic and often ironic use of a range of such conventional gender categories in ways that demonstrate their artificiality and the limitations they impose on men and women. Conrad's disruption of gender categories and use of hybrid forms allows him to critique the familiar structures of Victorian gender representation.

While readers rightfully associate Conrad with the adventure tradition and versions of the imperial romance, he specifically evokes a range of popular genres in his fiction, including detective and sensation fiction, genres which he similarly inhabits and effectively dismantles. Conrad's interest in detective fiction has been established by his use of the genre in *Chance* (1914) and *The Secret Agent*: Hampson (1980) persuasively reads *Chance* as detective fiction, noting Conrad's explicit use of its conventions, and, in an earlier study, I argue that, in the course of the investigation of the brutal death at the heart of the novel, *The Secret Agent* ironically realizes the disorder that classic detective fiction must repress to return to order (Harrington 1999). In *Joseph Conrad: A Personal Remembrance* (originally published in 1924), Conrad's friend and sometime collaborator Ford Madox Ford (1971) explains that Conrad read early sensation fiction during his time at sea. Ford describes Conrad as an avid reader of popular fiction, "such dog-eared books as are found in the professional quarters of ships' crews" including the unabashedly sensational works of Mary Elizabeth Braddon and Mrs. Henry Wood (96). Surveying Conrad's correspondence, Jones (1999) notes that Conrad continued to read Braddon and Wood later in life, and "while Conrad may have been critical of sensationalism, his own writing benefited from the tradition and commented on it" (193, 194).[2] Conrad's late fiction demonstrates his interest in sensation novels, especially their heroines and their conventional plots.

The Victorian detective story evolves alongside, and to some extent loosely overlaps with, the genre of sensation fiction; both forms are interested in the authoritative investigation of crimes or secrets and provide a requisite, reassuring return to order (the kind of resolution which W.H. Auden (1948) later describes as returning to a "state of grace," 150). Sensation fiction takes shape as a form in the early 1860s with Wilkie Collins's novel *The Woman in White* (1860) and Mary Elizabeth Braddon's *Lady Audley's Secret* (1862), both novels that center on illicit family secrets: "The best sensation novels are also, as Kathleen Tillotson points out 'novels with a secret,' or sometimes several secrets, in which new narrative strategies were developed to tantalise the reader by withholding information rather than divulging it" (Brantlinger 1982, 30). Rooted in the traditions of Gothic literature, sensation novels prominently feature women as victims, villains, or both, and, thus, frequently concern themselves with the injustice and victimization that women experience, sometimes titillating readers with ensuing rage or violence at the hands of women. Framing women's experience in the domestic setting, sensation novels often address gender in a contradictory way, legitimating women's concerns and critiquing their oppression while

---

[2] Jones (1999) establishes that Conrad's appreciation for these earlier popular women writers continued despite his "disparaging" view of the contemporary women writers Sarah Grand, Margaret Louisa Woods, and Marie Corelli (193).

reinscribing the necessity for patriarchal institutions and male steward-ship in a well-ordered ending. While such novels rarely directly express interest in women's sexuality and desire (for example, Mrs. Henry Wood's best-known novel *East Lynne* (1861) situates the adultery at the heart of the plot only as a regrettable past choice, absent from the text and without pleasure in remembrance), such issues surface in the frustra-tion, rage, and even greed expressed by the corrupted heroines of some of these novels.[3] As Conrad shifts his attention to genres typically cen-tered on female characters and marketed at women, he addresses their characteristic concerns with a skeptical eye, making their familiar plots strange with the contradiction and ambivalence that inform his work. Thus, Lena, the self-sacrificing lover in *Victory*, triumphs over Heyst's doubts in her last moments, vindicating her fantasy of understanding and idealized love, but this is only achieved in her death and spurs Heyst's suicide. Conrad rejects the Victorian happy marriage plot ending as well as the pretense that understanding and fulfillment can emerge from such characteristically circumscribed structures as the popular novel and the Victorian marriage.

Given sensation fiction's inherent focus on corruption and vice and the establishment of the genre contemporaneously with the publica-tion of Charles Darwin's *On the Origin of the Species* (1859), Conrad's engagement with sensation fiction dovetails with his interest in degen-eracy and contemporary criminal anthropology. It is in *The Secret Agent* that Conrad mentions popular criminal anthropologist Cesare Lombroso by name—early in the novel, Karl Yundt responds to Ossipon's evoca-tion of the pseudo-scientist, a reference Conrad shows to be reverent and lacking in self-awareness, with the disparaging dismissal "Lombroso is an ass" (47)—but readers will also recall the phrenological Belgian company doctor who cautions Marlow and asks to measure his head before his trip to the Congo in *Heart of Darkness*. In *Joseph Conrad and the Ethics of Darwinism: The Challenges of Science* (1983), Allan Hunter establishes Conrad's interest in Darwinism and criminal anthropology, tracing Conrad's treatment of Darwinian science through a range of Conrad's novels including *The Secret Agent*. Lombroso's ideas gained attention

---

[3] See Kathleen Montweiler's essay in *Beyond Sensation: Mary Elizabeth Braddon in Context* (2000) for a discussion of the conflation between greed and sexuality in *Lady Audley's Secret*.

in a late-Victorian society fascinated and disturbed by the possibilities of atavism and regression; interested in justifying and perpetuating hierarchies of gender, class, and race; and concerned with the problem of urban crime.[4] Lombroso used phrenological approaches, including cranial measurements and the classification of facial features, to classify criminals and thus develop a catalog of physical characteristics that serve as predictors for future criminal behavior; based on the assumption that all women and individuals from some ethnic groups were less evolved than the educated men who were his audience, Lombroso's work was strikingly racist and misogynist, assuming of woman as a category, "atavistically, she is nearer her origin than the male."[5] In *The Secret Agent*, Conrad uses direct references to Lombroso to draw attention to his ironic use of Lombrosian taxonomies throughout the novel, but I argue that Conrad's interest in the intersection of Darwinism, degeneracy, and gender is already evident in his early stories about "maternal passion"[6] "The Idiots" (1896) and "Amy Foster" (1901) and continues in much of Conrad's work from *Victory* onward. Conrad's self-conscious evocation of Lombrosian categories allows him to sketch and sometimes critique the bias that men like Kennedy in "Amy Foster," the captain in "A Smile of Fortune," or Ossipon—or even the typically generous and well-meaning Heyst—bring to considerations about women, and Conrad's use of such categories allows him to foreground gender and representation strategically in the late novels.

Notably, Conrad's treatment of the figure of the New Woman in *The Secret Agent* and *Chance* demonstrates a distrust of the politics of

---

[4] According to Hunter, Conrad could have become familiar with Lombroso's most influential work *Criminal Man* in its 1895 French translation, in partial translations, or in Havelock Ellis's influential book *The Criminal* (1890), since it was not fully translated from Italian into English until 1911 (Hunter 1983, 196–197). Lombroso's *The Female Offender* was translated into English in 1895 and thus would have been available to English-language readers (Rafter and Gibson 2004, 33).

[5] Nicole Hahn Rafter and Nicole Gibson (2004) argue that *The Female Offender* "constitutes perhaps the most extended proof of women's inferiority ever attempted" (32), and they note the intriguingly contradictory nature of Lombroso's argument that women are less evolved than men despite the fact that his female subjects show fewer of the kind of anatomical abnormalities that he believes are significant to crime and that women are much less likely to commit crimes (Lombroso and Ferraro 1915, 110–112).

[6] This term is used by Lombroso and Ferraro in *The Female Offender* (1915) (255), as well as by Conrad in the Author's Note to *The Secret Agent* (xii).

feminism: Winnie's supposedly liberated stint as a "free woman" in *The Secret Agent* is treated with brutal irony, since, as a Victorian woman, she cannot envision a life not lived in service to her brother and under the protection of a man.[7] Marlow's portrait of Mrs. Fyne, the feminist—and perhaps lesbian—mentor of young girls in *Chance*, is a mocking and scornful depiction of a self-interested and self-righteous woman. Both of these novels allude to the New Woman of the *fin de siècle*, a figure for the sexually and politically liberated woman who was broadly satirized and often associated with degenerates and aesthetes, and Conrad's derisory portrayals seem designed to situate these works self-consciously in opposition to a contemporary feminism that is implied to be strident and absurd.[8] However, Conrad's treatment of these figures reveals a more nuanced understanding of women's roles and situations, which, while it does not offset these images and others, complicates them. For all of Marlow's misogyny about Mrs. Fyne in *Chance*, he is complex and inconsistent in his gender politics, making reference to his feminine side and showing an ethical interest in the injustices Flora suffers addition to his personal interest in her. And if there is no viable possibility for women's liberation in the 1880s London society depicted so bleakly and ironically in *The Secret Agent*, it is hard to imagine a more damning portrait of the oppressive and infantilizing effects of traditional Victorian gender roles and assumptions than we find in Winnie's story.

It is Conrad's broader poetics, rife with subtlety, irony, and contradiction, mobile in perspective and often sharply self-aware, that informs his treatment of gender and his use of gendered representations, even as he expands his range of subjects and techniques in the late fiction. Those novels, long assumed to be lesser, commercially motivated works, still defy easy categorization, offering insight into the figures and the genres Conrad so powerfully exposes and critiques. The experimental approach

[7]See Brian Shaffer's (1995) treatment of Winnie as New Woman in "Domestic Ironies: Housekeeping as Mankeeping in *The Secret Agent*" and my discussion (Harrington 2007) in "The Female Offender, The New Woman, and Winnie Verloc in *The Secret Agent*."

[8]Though created in the 1890s in *The Woman's Herald* as a positive image for women of the coming twentieth century (Tusan 1998, 169), the term New Woman was often used pejoratively, a contradictory figure who was "a seductive temptress and a man-hater, over-educated and empty-headed, mannishly athletic or languidly anorexic" (Mitchell 1999, 583). So, Conrad's allusions to the New Woman in these novels fall into a familiar turn-of-the-century paradigm.

that such oppositional layers of representation imply is not in opposition to Conrad's best work and its characteristic modernism and should be considered requisite to our appreciation of his oeuvre.

Rather than surveying Conrad's works chronologically, this study groups them by feminine types, seeking to establish through Conrad's preoccupations with these figures and tropes the strains of repetition and allusion within his own work as he considers and refines these categories of representation. The very artificiality of these categories as Conrad constructs them might be seen to offer a marked critique of such categories and the figures and taxonomies from which they are derived, as Conrad works against the simplicity of polarized and superficial gendered representations he draws from popular literature and Victorian culture. Specifically, the focus of this book is Conrad's treatment of gender and genre as it emerges in a few of his early stories and coalesces in *The Secret Agent* in 1907, again surfacing in the later novels from *Chance* to *The Rover*, Conrad's last finished novel.[9] While the emphasis is on the late novels, I consider some earlier stories that address similar issues regarding gender and Victorian womanhood, borrowing and extending Hampson's perceptive reference to the "damaged women" who appear repeatedly in Conrad's late work.[10] In his portrayals of Flora in *Chance*, of Rita in *The Arrow of Gold*, of Arlette in *The Rover*, but also of Alice in "A Smile of Fortune," Amy in "Amy Foster," Susan of "The Idiots," Anne of "Because of the Dollars," and others, Conrad

---

[9] Of Conrad's novels after *The Secret Agent*, I do not address *Under Western Eyes* (1911), the short novel *The Shadow-Line* (1917), and *Suspense* (published posthumously in 1925). While fascinating and deserving of more scrutiny, Conrad's treatment of women in *Under Western Eyes* is indebted to Russian literary representation and politics to an extent that complicates its reading in the context of the Victorian gender representations that are the subject of this study. See Keith Carabine's chapter "The Dwindling of Natalia Haldin's 'Possibilities'" in *The Life and the Art: A Study of Conrad's* Under Western Eyes (1996), 128–173. *The Shadow-Line* more closely resembles Conrad's earlier fiction in form and content and is frequently considered in the context of Conrad's earlier work; the ship "like some rare women" is the strongest feminine presence in the novel (*SL* 49). Susan Jones's rich and engaging treatment of the incomplete manuscript *Suspense* in relation to the genre of the sensation novel stands as an insightful consideration of Conrad's use of Victorian popular fiction, one that has influenced this study. See Jones (1999), 194–220.

[10] In his essay "The Late Novels," Hampson (1996) notes, "Flora [in *Chance*] is the first of the damaged women of the late novels: she anticipates Lena in *Victory*, Rita in *The Arrow of Gold*, Arlette in *The Rover*, and perhaps even Adele in *Suspense* (146).

contemplates the damage caused by patriarchal structures, including the literary representations that influence the way women understand their positioning. For example, in *The Secret Agent*, the reader can experience the immediate degeneration of Winnie on the page as she comes to understand how and why Stevie's death transpired, yet Conrad also demonstrates that Winnie, walled up behind her impassive reserve, has been so damaged by the constrictions of her role as daughter, wife, and mother that she cannot envision any other future life than submission to a male protector or her gallows visions. While this is by no means an exhaustive study of women characters even in this subset of Conrad's work, the chapters in this book cover a range of representations that give us insight into Conrad's techniques and the complex significations of his own representations. Each of the female characters considered here is not only framed by Conrad in specific Victorian popular sensational, anthropological, and cultural discourses, but is also demonstrably damaged by the effects of such pervasive tropes of femininity. Conrad's representations of women demonstrate the illegitimacy of the patriarchal power to which these women are subject, reflecting the political consequences of these cultural paradigms for women and men.

Considering Conrad's relationship to Lombroso's categories, Chap. 2 of this study focuses on the ironic invocation of a kind of Lombrosian "maternal passion" in Conrad's early stories "The Idiots" and "Amy Foster," which disrupts male authority in the household; both stories chronicle the ways in which a mother brutally usurps her husband's presumed authority, preventing him from shaping the inheritance he will offer to his children. Conrad's ambivalent portrayal of maternal authority and women's degeneration renders the mothers darkly triumphant in rebellion, an unexpected departure from the role of the submissive wife. Addressing Conrad's use of pornography in *The Secret Agent* and other staged representations of women in *The Secret Agent* and *Victory*, Chap. 3 considers the ironic treatment of the family pornography shop in *The Secret Agent* and its unappealing merchandise as a kind of inversion of pornographic representation that serves to expose women's positioning in both novels as desirable commodities with a lack of autonomy in their lives. Conrad moves through a range of representations of women, portraying Lombrosian criminal anthropology as effectively pornographic and dismissing the political possibility of women's liberation as another artificial role foisted on women. Framing both women in sensational narratives, Conrad dramatizes the ways in which their choices are shaped by Victorian gender categories and the familiar representations that support those categories.

The following chapters focus specifically on iconic Victorian female figures to which Conrad returns in his fiction: the suicide, the fallen woman, the adulteress, and the embowered woman. In Chap. 4, I examine Conrad's repeated treatment of the female suicide from the early story "The Idiots," to *The Secret Agent*, and *Chance* as Conrad departs from the more familiar sentimentalized notion of the tragic woman from Victorian art and literature. The suicides in the former two texts, framed as the remedy to the impossible liberation provided by mariticide (as Conrad ironically refigures Victorian notions of the dishonored woman), contrast with Flora in *Chance*, who considers suicide repeatedly as a remedy to her sensationalized tragic role yet chooses to live. She ultimately fulfills a version of the happy marriage plot, even as the novel invites criticism of its conventionalized resolution, and Conrad's treatment of the figure of the female suicide reframes the disgrace of the initial image by legitimating the women's frustration with their conventional roles.

In Chap. 5, I return to *Victory* to address Conrad's treatment of the fallen woman in both that novel and *The Arrow of Gold*, considering the ways in which a male character's acculturation to manhood entails a reductive, categorical view of womanhood, which the novels reject. Both novels place women in threatening sexual economies that reduce them to besieged erotic objects, and the heroines flee with sympathetic men to an Edenic refuge whose privacy temporarily allows for a more egalitarian and sexually liberated space. Yet this newfound liberty is undermined by aspects of the sexual double standard from which the women fled, and Conrad shows men and women to be subject to similarly destructive illusions about gender roles and the expectations they raise in relationships. In Chap. 6, I consider another variation on the fallen woman figure, the unfaithful wife. Conrad's earlier Jamesian story "The Return" (1898) and his late novel *The Rescue* (1920) both consider the issue of women's dissatisfaction in marriage and the problematic possibility of adultery. Framed in the tropes of sensation fiction and featuring marriages based on illusion and presumption, Conrad initially poses extramarital relationships as a way for these heroines to escape to what may be a more equitable and affectionate union. Yet both "The Return" and *The Rescue* ultimately demonstrate that the heroines' frustration has less to do with their specific husbands than it does with the entrenched nature of their positioning as women that proves to be at the root of their dis-satisfaction. Chapter 7 considers a familiar representation of femininity that is literally as well as figuratively confined, the embowered woman in "A Smile of Fortune" and *The Rover* (1923). Through the familiar figure of the professional seaman, Conrad considers men's struggle with their problematic desires for women who are disgraced and embowered. These narratives show Alice and Arlette as objects of men's appraisal, attractive to men in part because of their isolation and psychological trauma, and Conrad makes explicit the disjunction between the women as figures of enchantment and the real circumstances of their lives, allowing Conrad to critique such enchanting representations even as he demonstrates their cultural dominance.

Conrad's resistance to works that are "well-wrought" and generically contained is evident throughout his career, as he crafts novels and characters that defy expectation, ably evoking and scrutinizing the conventions and presumptions of popular genres. Focusing attention on his use of representations of women allows us as readers to better understand Conrad's craft and technique later in his literary career as well as his treatment of gendered subjects, and it broadens our understanding of the politics of representation that underlie his aesthetic choices.

References

Auden, W.H. 1948. "The Guilty Vicarage." In *The Dyer's Hand and Other Essays*, 146–158. New York: Random House.

Baldwin, Debra Romanick. 2015. "Conrad and Gender". In *The New Cambridge Companion to Joseph Conrad*, ed. J.H. Stape, 132–146. Cambridge: Cambridge University Press.

Baxter, Katherine Isobel. 2010. *Joseph Conrad and the Swan Song of Romance*. Aldershot: Ashgate.

Braddon, Mary Elizabeth. 1862. *Lady Audley's Secret*. Leipzig: Bernard Tauchnitz.

Brantlinger, Patrick. 1982. "What Is 'Sensational' About the 'Sensation Novel'?". *Nineteenth-Century Fiction* 37 (1): 1–28.

Carabine, Keith. 1996. *The Life and the Art: A Study of Conrad's* Under Western Eyes. Amsterdam: Rodopi.

Collins, Wilkie. 1860. *The Woman in White*. London: Sampson Low, Son, and Co.

Conrad, Joseph. 1924. Author's Note to *The Secret Agent: A Simple Tale*, vii–xv. Garden City, NY: Doubleday, Page, and Company.

Erdinast-Vulcan, Daphna. 1999. *The Strange Short Fiction of Joseph Conrad: Writing, Culture, and Subjectivity*. Oxford: Oxford University Press.

Ford, Ford Madox. (1924) 1971. *Joseph Conrad: A Personal Remembrance*. New York: Octagon Books.

Hampson, Robert. 1980. "*Chance* and the Affair of the Purloined Brother." *The Conradian* 6 (2): 5–15.

———. 1992. *Joseph Conrad: Betrayal and Identity*. New York: St. Martin's Press.

———. 1996. "The Late Novels." In *The Cambridge Companion to Joseph Conrad*, ed. J.H. Stape, 140–159. Cambridge: Cambridge University Press.

Harrington, Ellen Burton. 1999. "'That Blood-Stained Inanity': Detection, Repression, and Conrad's *The Secret Agent*." *Conradiana* 31 (2): 114–119.

———. 2007. "The Female Offender, the New Woman, and Winnie Verloc in *The Secret Agent*." *The Conradian* 32 (1): 57–69.

Hunter, Allan. 1983. *Joseph Conrad and the Ethics of Darwinism: The Challenges of Science*. London: Croom Helm.

Jones, Susan. 1999. *Conrad and Women*. Oxford: Oxford University Press.

Kaplan, Carola M. 2005. "Beyond Gender: Deconstructions of Masculinity and Femininity from 'Karain' to *Under Western Eyes*." In *Conrad in the Twenty-First Century: Contemporary Approaches and Perspectives*, ed. Carola M. Kaplan, Peter Mallios, and Andrea White, 267–279. New York: Routledge.

Lombroso, Caesar, and William Ferraro (Lombroso, Cesare and Guglielmo Ferrero). 1915. *The Female Offender*. New York: Appleton and Co.

Mitchell, Sally. 1999. "New Woman, Old and New." *Victorian Literature and Culture*: 579–588.

Montweiler, Katherine. 2000. "Marketing Sensation: Lady Audley's Secret and Consumer Culture". In *Beyond Sensation: Mary Elizabeth Braddon in Context*, ed. Marlene Tromp, Pamela K. Gilbert, and Aeron Haynie, 43–62. Albany, NY: State University of New York Press.

Moser, Thomas. 1966. *Joseph Conrad: Achievement and Decline*. Hamden, CT: Archon Books.

Nadelhaft, Ruth. 1991. *Joseph Conrad*. Atlantic Highlands, NJ: Humanities Press International.

Rafter, Nicole Hahn, and Mary Gibson. 2004. Introduction to *Criminal Woman, the Prostitute, and the Normal Woman*, ed. Cesare Lombroso and Guglielmo Ferrero, 3–33. Durham: Duke University Press.

Schneider, Lissa. 2003. *Conrad's Narratives of Difference: Not Exactly Tales for Boys*. New York: Routledge.

Shaffer, Brian. 1995. "Domestic Ironies: Housekeeping as Mankeeping in *The Secret Agent*." In *Keeping the Victorian House: A Collection of Essays*, ed. Vanessa D. Dickerson, 313–329. New York: Garland.

Simmons, Allan. 2000. "Feminist Approaches". In *Oxford Reader's Companion to Conrad*, ed. Owen Knowles, and Gene M. Moore, 109–110. Oxford: Oxford University Press.

Straus, Nina Pelikan. 1987. "The Exclusion of the Intended from Secret Sharing in Conrad's 'Heart of Darkness'". *Novel: A Forum on Fiction* 20 (2): 123–137.

Tusan, Michelle Elizabeth. 1998. "Inventing the New Woman: Print Culture and Identity Politics during the Fin-de-Siècle". *Victorian Periodicals Review* 31 (2): 169–182.

Wood, Mrs. Henry (Ellen). 1861. *East Lynne*. Leipzig: Bernhard Tauchnitz.

CHAPTER 2

The Passionate Mother and the Contest for Authority: "The Idiots" and "Amy Foster"

In the early stories "The Idiots" (1896) and "Amy Foster" (1901), Conrad ambivalently portrays the heroines as figures of sensational rebellion, as each chooses to resist the requisite submission of the wifely role and assume parental authority. Offering an ironic rejection of the Victorian happy marriage plot, each story trains an almost anthropological eye on the consequences of both financial and genetic inheritance and highlights the fearful regression of its female protagonist as she lashes out against her spouse. Conrad's stories here intertwine representations of Darwinian degeneracy culled from criminal anthropology with degenerate tropes from popular literature, and, in his unsettling conclusions, Conrad ends with a degree of unmitigated wifely frustration that challenges the Victorian marital hierarchy.

Superficially, "The Idiots" and "Amy Foster" have little in common: the former, an oft-denigrated—denigrated even by Conrad himself in his 1920 Author's Note to *Tales of Unrest* (1924a)[1] —melodramatic story that is a distant rendering of a family tragedy culminating in mariticidal murder; the latter, a much appreciated, biographically tinged tale of a castaway's ultimate rejection by his once-generous wife, which is seen through the eyes of a dominating narrator. However, "The Idiots" and "Amy Foster"

---

[1] Conrad comments with palpable irritation, "'The Idiots' is such an obviously derivative piece of work that it is impossible for me to say anything about it here. The suggestion of it was not mental but visual: the actual idiots" (*TU* ix).

© The Author(s) 2017
E.B. Harrington, *Conrad's Sensational Heroines*,
DOI 10.1007/978-3-319-63297-1_2

recast and critique the ideal of family life by exposing the shortcomings of conventional parental and spousal roles that subjugate wives, using the family circle to explore both the atavism resulting from the stresses of familial conflict and the inescapable influence of genetic inheritance in determining identity. Conrad here makes much of the way apparently civilized individuals have the potential to regress, relying on instinct and violence rather than consideration to determine their behavior, and, by emphasizing the resemblances between the generations, he shows inherited traits to be a significant influence on identity. Each story culminates in a dramatic overthrow of paternal authority in the household that leaves the reader with a powerful and disturbing rendering of maternal authority. In "The Idiots" and "Amy Foster," Conrad (1924b, 1925) depicts the irony in the failure of patriarchal culture to ensure the father's legacy, and he does so without glorying in the triumph of the mother; indeed, both stories end with a particularly bleak vision of the future.

Richard Herndon (1960) describes the correspondence between the seemingly dissimilar husbands in the two stories: "Despite his marriage, he still feels isolated, discerns a hostility in his surroundings, has conflicts with his neighbors, and desires a child through whom he can escape his isolation" (555, 562). The desire to use fatherhood as a remedy for isolation, to give meaning to the father's existence, brings these men into direct—ultimately deadly—conflict with their spouses. The degeneracy that is ascribed to the mothers might be read as an embodiment of turn-of-the-century anxieties about women's liberation and their potential threat to the dominance of men, even as Conrad casts the men as brutish or childish in ways that undermine the idealization of that dominance. Indeed, the rural towns in which the stories are set embody the broader failings of a patriarchal society that recasts its prejudices as a natural hierarchy, failing to recognize that degeneracy cannot be ascribed simply to the disabled or the foreign. In Conrad's telling, degeneracy is endemic, a perspective which he enlarges upon in *The Secret Agent*.

Initially, "The Idiots" chronicles the disruption of a bourgeois farmer's ambitious plans for his land and inheritance by the birth of four mentally disadvantaged children, but when Jean-Pierre Bacadou's otherwise conventional wife, Susan, murders him with her "long scissors" as he tries to rape her in the hope of conceiving an unafflicted fifth child, Conrad shows the way their contrasting parental assumptions lead to mortal conflict (*TU* 1924b, 76). To Jean-Pierre, another child is the hope of the future of his farm, but, to Susan Bacadou, a fifth child will

only add to the unbearable household burden of four wholly dependent children who do not recognize her, another reminder of her failure
as a mother. Ultimately, the whole family—not just the children—shows
signs of degeneracy, particularly in what might be read as a darkly comic
rendering of Lombrosian maternal passion, a perspective that "Amy
Foster" also recalls.

There, the intelligent and cosmopolitan Dr. Kennedy offers a with-
ering description of the "dull," degenerate Amy Foster that shows her
to be undeserving of Yanko Goorall, her attractive, yet markedly foreign, castaway husband (*TOS* 107). Her abandonment of Yanko in what
proves to be his final illness demonstrates her cruelty as she flees, ele-
mentally fearful of the influence Yanko desires over their infant son and
finally representative of the kind of xenophobic intolerance that she initially countered. Yet her fear hinges on his desire to assert his paternal
rights, since rather than fully assimilate to his new home, he desires to
form a bond with his son exclusive of Amy that will allow him to pass
on the prayers, dances, and other cultural practices of his homeland that
he misses terribly. This community with his son will presumably exclude
Amy, who deeply fears these delirious lapses into his native language during his illness. Kennedy's final image of Amy characterizes her as "hanging over" the child who has the "fluttered air of a bird caught in a snare"
(142). Notably, this image is used twice to describe Yanko in the text,
once when he's first discovered after the shipwreck and once in his final
illness, and it here reaffirms the loaded image of Amy as the victor in
a crude parental contest for possession of the child, a "dull brain[ed]"
mother that has unfairly displaced a deserving father (126, 141, 142).
In its own way, each story chronicles the way in which a mother brutally
seizes domestic control and blocks her husband's authority to determine
what inheritance he will proffer.

This interest in survival and inheritance runs through much of
Conrad's writing; as Allan Hunter (1983) explains, Conrad's fiction uses
a scientific model in its ethical consideration, "testing [theories], explor-
ing them and eventually re-writing some of them by comparing them to
reality again" (6).[2] The quasi-science of Lombroso's racist and misogynist
tomes, including *The Female Offender* (Lombroso and Ferraro 1915),

---

[2] Hunter (1983) establishes Conrad's interest in Darwinian thinking, including the influence
of late-century criminal anthropologist Cesare Lombroso on Conrad's novel *The Secret Agent*.

serves as a kind of ironic touchstone for *The Secret Agent*. The novel's characterization of Winnie might recall in particular Lombroso's ideas from *The Female Offender* about crimes of passion resulting from maternal love. This idealized, problematic envisioning of maternal love and its criminal manifestations also speaks to the conflicted relationships in "The Idiots" and "Amy Foster."[3] In both tales, mothers act out with fear and hostility against their husbands, inviting Myrtle Hooper's (1996) reading of "Amy Foster": "Yanko's threat implicates [Amy's] role as mother, indeed sets in opposition her roles as mother and wife, as she understands them; roles both central to her self" (60). We might read this as a commentary on the vexed gender relations in both stories, which Conrad frames through sensationalized female figures. Amy's abandonment of Yanko is cast as a kind of quiet violence that allows her to usurp his parental role, an allusion to the conniving, hypocritical wife of Victorian melodrama. In "The Idiots," Susan also experiences a conflict of roles in which she violently refuses her husband's authority; her fear of having another disabled child is so powerful that she defies marital, civic, and religious authority in killing her husband, and she believes herself justified in so doing. Susan's transition from faithful wife to killer recalls those sensational heroines like Braddon's Lady Audley, whose placid exterior might conceal violent rage and possibly madness. Conrad balances the potential justification for both mothers' behavior against their obvious degeneration and the fearsome consequences of their actions.

I

"The Idiots" invites a Darwinian reading from its very first images, its merciless glimpse of the children, presented as something of a sight-seeing landmark for the traveler who initially narrates the story. The impressionist view of the farm "resembling the unskilful daubs of a naïve picture" yields a series of images of the children: "The imbecile face was red, and the bullet head with close-cropped hair seemed to lie alone, its chin in the dust"; "And he stood with [...] his head sunk between the shoulders, all hunched up in the flood of heat"; "The imperfect thing

---

[3] Hugh Epstein (1991) notes the apparent connection between "The Idiots" and *The Secret Agent*, since the earlier story seems to work through much of the domestic plot that emerges in the novel, focusing on the ultimately murderous tensions between a husband and wife responsible for an "idiot" child or children.

that lived within them moved those beings to howl at us"; "The faces were purple with the strain of yelling" (56–58). The narrator also mentions the "misshapen brain of the creature," characterizing the children as "an offense to the sunshine" (57, 58). The inescapable, physical descriptions of the children's apparent degeneracy, their "idiocy" in the parlance of the town, set the tone for the story, which hinges on the fundamental irony that the community is suffused with idiocy for which the children ultimately serve as scapegoats of a sort; as Daniel Schwarz (1969) notes in a defense of the story, "the blighted offspring are stark symbols, rather than the natural effects, of a community where the family, clerical, and political structures are undermined by the hypocrisy, selfishness and vanity of those in positions to provide moral leadership" (113). The focus on inheritance and familial connections in "The Idiots" reminds us that Jean-Pierre and Susan Bacadou are not just the parents of blighted offspring; they are, of course, blighted offspring themselves.

The plot begins with Jean-Pierre's insistence to his father that he succeed to his family's farmland. Though this is the natural order, there is something brutal in his assertion of the filial succession; this insistence of his new family's right becomes increasingly ironic as his wife bears a series of children unfit to take over the farm and her husband is more concerned with the land, his birthright, than he is concerned with the children themselves. As Claude Maisonnat (2002) explains, "the focus [of the story] is unmistakably on the problematics of filiation, generation, in relation to the land, and the story raises the more fundamental questions of the definition of subjectivity and identity," questions that shake Jean-Pierre's self-image and expectations as powerfully as his wife's (54).

The story abounds in Conradian ironies, as Susan's initial elation at the birth of her children is tinged with concern about how others view her: "Susan was happy, too, for she did not want to be spoken of as the unfortunate woman, and now she had children no one could call her that" (61). When Jean-Pierre hears the whispers in the market, he goes to confront his wife, as though he had not noticed the children's arrested development himself. Her role is defined against his indifference: "The mother watched with other eyes; listened with otherwise expectant ears. [...] Her mind remained by the cradle, night and day on the watch, to hope and suffer" (63–64). This third child is like the twins, and their disability is defined through their lack of ability to interact with the mother. Susan suffers from their lack of reciprocation; her children do not know her or appreciate her, and she knows that others know her as the mother of the "idiot" children, even more an "unfortunate" than she initially feared (61).

As the story proceeds, both Jean-Pierre and Susan show signs of degeneration, prefigured in the mental regression experienced by their fathers. Despite the fact that the proud Republican Jean-Pierre "sold his soul" to the church in an act of desperation (67), his last child is like the others, and the previously temperate man takes to drink and violence, even striking his wife. Jean-Pierre, a conventional peasant farmer, stolid and indifferent, once temperate and proud of his prospects and his farm, degenerates in the narrative until, desperate for his hope of the future to return, he decides to rape his wife in the hope of conceiving another child. While this clearly represents an atavistic regression on the part of the husband, Conrad's naturalistic vision of a peasant farmer so strained by his failure to maintain control and fulfill his paternal ambitions that he will dominate his wife violently to ensure succession, the narrative also depicts the regression of Susan as the narrative shows her current state against the flashback she is reliving.

When Susan enters her mother's establishment with the "half-aloud" cry of "Mother!" trancelike and traumatized after murdering Jean-Pierre, her mother recalls that her husband had mental illness and fears its resurgence in her daughter, looking for the paternal hereditary pathway to exculpate herself (73). As she later exclaims, "You wicked woman—you disgrace me. But there! You always resembled your father" (76). The implication is that, presumably, any inherited problems with the children must have descended from the "deranged" grandfather and not from her (74). Susan has hitherto appeared to be a compliant housewife, but her marital issue has made sex unnatural and revolting to her, not a conduit for redemption as Jean-Pierre hopes, but a maternal curse.

Cesare Lombroso's work famously asserts that criminals are atavistic, a kind of evolutionary throwback, and as he considers the causes of women's delinquency, he argues that women are not just less evolved than men, but that they resemble children in some ways (Rafter and Gibson 2004, 7, 9). When Lombroso studies "offenses committed through maternal love" in the chapter on "Crimes of Passion" in *The Female Offender*, he notes their rarity, since mothers do not want to risk separation from their children: "Almost the only person against whom they have to be protected is a bad or careless father, and he fortunately is not a very common phenomenon, elementary duty to his family not being the relation in which the civilized male shows himself most frequently wanting" (Lombroso and Ferraro 1915, 255). In this, the criminal anthropologist presents a normative version of the parental roles, assuming that a mother's love (at least for her small children) generally acts as what he calls a "moral prophylactic against crime and evil" and that the father recognizes his duty to the family (Lombroso and Ferraro 1915, 254–255). Since Conrad elsewhere both borrows and satirizes Lombrosian taxonomies of the kind found in *The Female Offender* (notably in *The Secret Agent*), I argue that we might read "The Idiots" as a rendering of the kind of maternal passion that Lombroso contemplates as a cause of crime. We witness Susan's degeneration, cast as a kind of evolutionary regression, through her shock after Jean-Pierre's murder. While Jean-Pierre fulfills some version of Lombroso's "bad and careless father" in the story, one whose "neglect of paternal responsibility" extends to conceiving children solely in the hope that they might serve his ambition (Lombroso and Ferraro 1915, 255; Moore 1997, 54), Lombroso clearly envisions crimes of maternal passion as being protective of existing children, not effected to prevent other children from being conceived. Conrad's plot here undermines the ideal of parenthood that even Lombroso presumes in considering crimes of passion committed for reasons of "maternal and domestic love" (Lombroso and Ferraro 1915, 253), as Conrad offers us a maternal passion that is self-serving rather than altruistic. Both parents in Conrad's story are more wrapped up in their own fears and ambitions than what is best for the children, and Susan characterizes her resentment in terms of her "accursed" role as mother rather than compassion for her children (*TU* 126). At the end of the story, she longs to justify the rightness of her actions.

II

The reader is invited to compare the two mothers as, fittingly in the story's dark irony, Susan's mother rejects Susan as a cause of shame as well: "I wish you had died little. I will never dare to show my old head in the sunshine again. There are worse misfortunes than idiot children. I wish you had been born to me simple—like your own" (129). In the climactic scene, Susan, haunted by her husband's visage, flees across the bottom of the rocky bay as the tide is just beginning to come in. Bystanders regard her fearfully and several call her an "accursed thing" as she has apparently devolved to resemble her children, an ending that recalls Lombroso's evolutionary considerations, albeit filtered through

Conrad's own melodramatic vision (133). Fleeing help as she relives the murder of her husband in the encroaching tide, she falls struggling into the rising water and dies.

The story ends with a vision of absurd domestic violence as the selfish parents die to leave custody of their children to their grandmother. As Hugh Epstein (1991) explains in his consideration of the two stories, "The vision of man in this tale is of a diminished creature who is not at home in his habitat, the potential tragedy in the story of patrimony receiving a sardonically reductive treatment. Conrad is almost comically unable to write the story of a woman's self-determination" (222). This vision of liberation, one in which a woman uses violence to free herself from a union which she perceives as unjust, cannot generate freedom in "The Idiots," since, in Conrad's ironic rendering, women are shown to be ideologically bound by the conventions of patriarchal society even after they murder their spouses.

In addition to its shared interest in spousal roles and familial conflict, "Amy Foster" offers a similar social critique to "The Idiots." Keith Carabine (1992) notes that, like *The Secret Agent*, "Amy Foster" "is calculated to shock [Conrad's] English reading public into a recognition of the limitations of their social codes, of their insularity, and of the thinness of the protections they build against the invasion of the strange and alien" (196). Richard Ruppel (1996) extends this reading, characterizing "Amy Foster" as "a colonialist story in reverse" and describing Kennedy's "almost anthropological tone" borrowed from colonialist fiction in which the British subjects become the natives under critique (126, 128, 130). This anthropological bent in the narrator, Dr. Kennedy, confirms his superior, outsider's viewpoint; while he is hardly as problematic as the darkly comic figure of Ossipon in *The Secret Agent*, he also presents himself as a scientific authority interested in distancing himself from those he views as inferior by diagnosing them.

Kennedy is described by the narrator to whom Kennedy tells the story as a highly appealing figure, an engaging conversationalist with a big laugh, immediately before the initial, lackluster description of Amy: "I had the time to see her dull face, red, not with a mantling blush, but as if her flat cheeks had been vigorously slapped, and to take in the squat figure, the scanty, dusty brown hair drawn into a tight knot at the back of the head" (*TOS* 107). This description seems to invite the reader to judge her as degraded or shamed rather than merely embarrassed. When the narrator comments to Kennedy, "She seems a dull creature," he develops the description in an invitingly quasi-scientific analysis: "She is very passive. It's enough to look at the red hands hanging at the end of those short arms, at those slow, prominent brown eyes, to know the inertness of her mind" (107). Her passivity, short arms, and "slow, prominent" eyes emphasize her brutish quality, as Kennedy clearly sees her as inferior and undeveloped (107). Kennedy, whose "papers on the fauna and flora made him known to scientific societies," adopts a condescending, misogynist tone to Amy, as another subject for what the narrator describes as the "penetrating power of his mind" (106). Certainly, Kennedy's point of view, at least with regard to Amy, seems to uphold the Lombrosian premise that women are less evolutionarily advanced; while also problematically childlike in Kennedy's portrayal, Yanko's behavior and vision of what constitutes civilized society are sanctioned by the more sophisticated Kennedy. Yanko's situation causes him to be more self-aware than Amy, though Yanko's ability to understand the new society into which he is thrust clearly has its limitations. In her essay, "'Amy Foster' and the Blindfolded Woman," Eve Whittaker (2007) reads Amy against Dr. Kennedy's portrayal, which she describes as "accurate observation, along with incorrect interpretation" (253). Certainly, Kennedy's judgments about and analysis of Amy heavily influence the narrator's perspective on her and form a significant part of the story's focus.

Perhaps it is her monotonous life in part that leads to Amy's "possession" by Yanko; he is notably the more attractive of the couple in Kennedy's eyes, though he speculates that Amy's compassion, her "golden heart, and soft to people's misery" as Yanko describes it, makes her attractive to her husband (133). Interestingly, Amy's father also made a problematic marriage, one that caused him to lose his position and inheritance, so Amy is repeating a family mistake, though this marital error will actually prove materially successful for her unlike her father. With Swaffer, the avid collector of "outlandish" things who has taken Yanko in, he has a paternalistic, even "feudal" relationship, and appropriately, it is through Swaffer that, in some sense, Yanko regains his lost birthright (127, 136). He can never go home to the Carpathian Mountains because of the family property that was sold to purchase his passage, but by saving the life of Swaffer's grandchild with no expectation of recompense he earns a cottage and an acre of land for his marriage.

Despite his gains in property and marriage, Yanko never fully adapts to the social norms of the area. He cannot get the village men to join in his songs or accept his dances over a pint, and his household remains isolated, as evidenced by the fact that "nobody seems to care to come" to sit with Yanko during his illness to spell Amy as his care-taker (139). Finally, as Whittaker observes, "The birth of his son seems to give [Yanko] the good news that he doesn't *have* to adapt" (265), since he can create a community with his son. What seems like a natural impulse on Yanko's part creates "unreasonable terror" in his wife, and it is clear that she has come to value the baby over her husband (139). In Lombrosian terms, her maternal love now predominates over conju-gal love, and she fears for her child's safety in the face of what she con-strues as the foreign nature of her husband. In her mind, he has become a version of Lombroso's "bad or careless" father against whom she must protect the child. Kennedy offers another capsule analysis of her char-acter: "I wondered whether his difference, his strangeness, were not penetrating with repulsion that dull nature they had begun irresistibly attracting," and later, "I looked into her shortsighted eyes, at her dumb eyes that once in her life had seen an enticing shape, but, seemed, star-ing at me, to see nothing at all now" (Lombroso and Ferraro 1915, 255; *TOS* 137–139). Again, her imperceptive, brutish nature is established; in Kennedy's narration, Amy operates solely on base instinct, her attrac-tion and repulsion both equally strong and lacking in self-awareness. She abandons Yanko to his fever and his death apparently because of this same overpowering instinct: she flees when he tries "to get to her round the table," and she senses a physical threat (140). Kennedy describes the "dull, blurred glance" that he could not have glimpsed himself and seems to depict her as regressing into an animal state of fear (140).

Amy's initial actions to Yanko bespeak a nobleness of character and capacity to sympathize, which Kennedy describes as affiliated with imagi-nation, that we must then reconcile with Kennedy's portrait of her as atavistic. Kennedy is intrigued by her act of compassion and imagination, while he seems to find her attraction to the "good-looking" Yanko (124) both unusual for her closed community and quite natural and instinctual, since Yanko attracts him as well. Yet, while his sympathy for and interest in Yanko persists to the end of the story, Kennedy has simply discounted Amy, as though she has regressed to an expected, baser character that ceases to be engaging. Whittaker (2007) puts the plot and its ending in purely evolutionary terms, which means that Yanko is actually a "success-ful male" in terms of evolution, since he survived the shipwreck to pass on his genes unlike his companions and that "Amy personifies evolution-ary ruthlessness in the female" (263, 264). Despite Yanko's untimely

death, his offspring survives, and Amy's rejection of Yanko may be justified by the notion that, in her judgment at least, it has helped ensure
their son's survival. Certainly, Yanko's inability to understand fully his
neighbors' perceptions of him and how they judge him and his inability or refusal to adapt to life in Colebrook mark him as an outsider, the
kind of man that Kennedy as an intellectual, a traveler and naturalist,
would want to mythologize. Yanko is evidence of the narrow mindset
that Kennedy does not share and that comes to be exemplified by Amy.
Kennedy does not see her idiosyncrasies as admirable as he does with
Yanko; Kennedy cannot read Amy's motivations as simply as Yanko's, so
he assumes they signal her degradation. In presenting the tale through
Kennedy's eyes, Conrad's story invites us to imagine the limitations of
his perspective, colored by his sometimes self-serving values, and this
opens up a larger critique of society's judgments, the very society from
which Kennedy seeks to distinguish himself with his seemingly progres-
sive perspective. Certainly, denigrating Amy seems to be Kennedy's reaction to society's rejection of Yanko. Informed of Yanko's death, Amy's
father comments, "I don't know that it isn't for the best," and the child
becomes simply "Amy Foster's boy" (141–142).

"The Idiots and "Amy Foster" offer ironic, even darkly comic, treat-
ments of mothers' usurpation of the paternal rights over progeny and
determining inheritance. The stories present the notion of inheritance,
meaning received property and culture as well as traits, and the right to
pass those on, as constitutive of masculinity in these fathers. Thus, these
instances of aggressive mother love are powerfully emasculating even
beyond their deadly import, since they terminate the father's desired
legacy of influence on his children. The stories probe the late-Victorian
anxieties that result from the renegotiation of family life that must occur
as mothers come to see themselves as increasingly politically empowered
and potentially angry, recalling the suppressed feminine rage that is at
the heart of so many of those sensational novels structured around a
woman's secret. They also demonstrate the ways in which fathers long
to possess their children and shape them in their own image, inviting a
larger critique of patriarchal culture. These portraits of family life thus
connect to the broad social critique in the stories, which consider the
ways that communities scapegoat the foreign and the disabled, using
such labels to support the self-serving pretense of a unified society.

Presenting an ambivalent portrait of parental conflict and maternal dominance, the stories also undermine any idealization of women's

liberation in these atavistic portrayals, though they frankly portray the limitations of the wifely role. When Susan Bacadou reassures herself, "Dead men have no children" (*TU* 79), as she is confronted by the delusion of her dead husband which haunts her in the last minutes of her life, the hollowness of her bitter triumph resounds. Amy's dominance is more marked; she ends the story in sole possession of the cottage and property and is able to raise her son as she wishes, her abandonment of her foreign husband sanctioned by her community. The struggle to survive and propagate extends in these tales even to the family circle, wherein husbands cannot assume that physical dominance will ensure their survival or the survival of their values in the next generation. In depicting these rebellious—and even violent—mothers, Conrad evokes the transgressive tropes of the sensational heroine, even as he rejects the sentimental resolutions of such novels. Thus, he highlights the confining nature of such representations and the oppressive gender roles they signify, demonstrating the alarming ways in which mother instinct can check paternal authority.

REFERENCES

Carabine, Keith. 1992. 'Irreconcilable Differences': England as an Undiscovered Country' in Conrad's 'Amy Foster'. In *The Ends of the Earth: 1876–1918*, ed. Simon Gatrell, 187–204. London: Ashfield.

Conrad, Joseph. 1924a. Author's Note to *Tales of Unrest*, vii–ix. Garden City, NY: Doubleday, Page, and Company.

———. 1924b. "The Idiots." In *Tales of Unrest*, 93–142. Garden City, NY: Doubleday, Page, and Company.

———. 1925. "Amy Foster." In *Typhoon and Other Stories*, 105–142. Garden City, NY: Doubleday, Page, and Company.

Epstein, Hugh. 1991. 'Where He Is Not Wanted': Impression and Articulation in 'The Idiots' and 'Amy Foster'. *Conradiana: A Journal of Joseph Conrad Studies* 23 (3): 217–232.

Herndon, Richard. 1960. The Genesis of Conrad's 'Amy Foster'. *Studies in Philology* 57: 549–566.

Hooper, Myrtle. 1996. 'Oh, I Hope He Won't Talk': Narrative and Silence in 'Amy Foster'. *Conradian* 21 (2): 51–64.

Hunter, Allan. 1983. *Joseph Conrad and the Ethics of Darwinism: The Challenges of Science*. London: Croom Helm.

Lombroso, Caesar, and William Ferraro (Lombroso, Cesare and Guglielmo Ferrero). 1915. *The Female Offender*. New York: Appleton and Co.

Maisonnat, Claude. 2002. The Venomous Sibillation of Subdued Words: Literary Heterosis and Generic Crossbreeding in 'The Idiots'. *Epoque Conradienne* 28: 43–59.

Moore, Gene M. 1997. Conrad's 'The Idiots' and Maupassant's 'La Mère au monstres.' In *Conrad Intertexts and Appropriations: Essays in Memory of Yves Hervouet*, ed. Gene M. Moore, Owen Knowles, and J.H. Stape, 49–58. Amsterdam, Netherlands: Rodopi.

Rafter, Nicole Hahn, and Mary Gibson. 2004. Introduction to *Criminal Woman, the Prostitute, and the Normal Woman*, by Cesare Lombroso and Guglielmo Ferrero, 3–33. Durham: Duke University Press.

Ruppel, Richard. 1996. Yanko Goorall in the Heart of Darkness: 'Amy Foster' as Colonialist Text. *Conradiana* 28 (2): 126–132.

Schwarz, Daniel. 1969. Moral Bankruptcy in Ploumar Parish: A Study of Conrad's 'The Idiots'. *Conradiana* 1 (3): 113–117.

Whittaker, Eve. 2007. 'Amy Foster' and the Blindfolded Woman. *Conradiana: A Journal of Joseph Conrad Studies* 39 (3): 249–272.

CHAPTER 3

Pornography and Representations
of Women: *The Secret Agent* and *Victory*

*The primitive woman was rarely a murderess; but she was always a prostitute,
and such she remained until semi-civilized epochs.*
—Lombroso and Ferraro in *The Female Offender* (1915, 111)

Joseph Conrad's novel *The Secret Agent* (1924b) frames the narrative with
images of pleasure, eroticism, and stimulation that are already suffused
with ennui: storefront pornography comprised in part of "faded, yellow
dancing girls," "ancient French comic publications," and other dubious
pleasures; aged anarchist publications and aged anarchists incapable of
rousing anyone; a bomb trigger always kept in a trousers pocket that is
only to be caressed and contemplated, never detonated in the text (5, 3).
The bomb blast of real consequence is, of course, detonated accidentally
at the wrong spot. Naturally, it is no accident that *The Secret Agent* opens
in the seedy Brett Street pornography shop that serves as the Verloc family business and the entry to the family domicile. Like so many seemingly
scintillating threads of the narrative, this one proves to be something of
a sham, since the shop's pornography appears to be as indifferent as its
anarchist newspapers; indeed, both stimulate such little enthusiasm and
elicit so little demand that the shop can only be considered an "ostensible
business" since the sexualized representations of women, the racy novels,
and the political publications Verloc stocks can be considered at best only
superficially transgressive (3).

© The Author(s) 2017   31
E.B. Harrington, *Conrad's Sensational Heroines*,
DOI 10.1007/978-3-319-63297-1_3

Yet, in another sense, these "more or less undressed dancing girls," images of women performing for pay turned into the aged and undesirable wares of a sham establishment, are very much at the center of Conrad's resonant critique of Victorian representations of women and their characteristic gender roles in *The Secret Agent* and *Victory* (*SA* 5). In *The Secret Agent*, Conrad depicts pornography—in the ways it objectifies, frames, and eroticizes its subjects—as an analog for contemporary criminal anthropology. Conrad's fiction sets these pornographic representations and anthropological taxonomies against representations of the liberated woman, a figure that could be seen as a kind of remedy to women's circumscribed roles that offers women more autonomy. However, Conrad portrays women's liberation as farcical in these novels, where it serves as merely another preordained role to which women might conform, analogous to these other categories. In his depiction of women as sexual commodities in these novels, Conrad emphasizes the ways in which women's subjugation to generic roles evokes prostitution much more than liberation.

Conrad self-consciously foregrounds generic representations of women in *The Secret Agent* and *Victory*, for example, inviting the reader to imagine the photograph of one of the "faded, yellow dancing girls" from the Verlocs' pornography shop, only good enough to be sold "to an amateur, as though she had been alive and young," set against the youthful Winnie, who is described as both curvaceous and frustratingly self-contained amidst the less-than-lascivious wares of the family shop (*SA* 5).[1] This juxtaposition immediately highlights Winnie's sexuality and, in retrospect, the extent to which sex for her is part of a socially sanctioned and negotiable bargain, one linked not to pleasure but to business. This gesture also indicates a broader move on Conrad's part, as he alludes to a range of familiar representations of women from the nineteenth century and the *fin de siècle*, including pornography, criminal anthropology, and popular fiction, and reframes them in ways that highlight both the oppressive nature of these roles and their cultural influence on individual men and women. Given the conventional perspectives of Winnie of *The Secret Agent* and Lena of *Victory*, neither woman is able

---

[1] Conrad places Winnie and her wares in proximity in the shop and in the language of novel itself, as we read from the end of the novel's sixth paragraph to the beginning of its seventh.

to envision liberty from the gendered constraints that structure their lives. Both heroines have been previously victimized by men and use their beauty and sexuality to form alliances with older men who can offer them security and stability, pragmatically acknowledging their status as goods that they must negotiate to survive.

In both *The Secret Agent* and *Victory*, Conrad starkly emphasizes the extent to which Winnie and Lena are bound tragically by these sensationalized roles. Winnie cannot be liberated by killing her husband as a kind of murderous New Woman, and Lena cannot create a new life on a desert island without the burden of her sexuality intruding to push her into a familiar narrative of feminine self-sacrifice. In portraying these women's struggles with their limited choices and roles, both novels link sexuality to violence, alluding to the victimized and victimizing heroines of Victorian sensation novels and to discourses on degeneracy at the *fin de siècle*. Conrad's irony fundamentally shapes the perspective of these novels, since the novels paradoxically both inhabit and critique patriarchal structures from phrenology and popular culture. While it is clear that Conrad does not envision any kind of meaningful personal liberation for women, these novels evoke representations of women from Victorian culture and popular literature to portray women's personal disenfranchisement and servitude in ways that are deeply critical of nineteenth-century discourses about gender.

I

In his 1920 "Author's Note" to *The Secret Agent*, Conrad (1924a) describes the novel as Winnie's story, as he looks back at the novel and finally compares himself to a kind of anarchist bomber: "I confess that it makes a grisly skeleton. But still I will submit that telling Winnie Verloc's story to its anarchistic end of utter desolation, madness, and despair, and telling it as I have told it here, I have not intended to commit a gratuitous outrage on the feelings of mankind" (*SA* xv). Despite the author's implicit relish in the rhetorical flourish at the end of this passage (the last line of his Author's Note), the emphasis on the literary outrage he may have committed unintentionally characterizes the mischievous nature of Conrad's ironic enterprise in this novel. By claiming Winnie as the center of the novel, performing a kind of substitution for, or at least an inversion of, the expectations set up at the outset of the novel, Conrad invites us as readers to shift our attention to the unremarkable-seeming woman who commits the ultimate outrage against her wifely role; in one sense, the rest of the novel builds bit by bit the circumstantial and psychological basis for Winnie's murder of Verloc and her subsequent suicide. When Conrad refers to the writing of this novel as "simply attending to my business," there is a sense in which he registers a comparison between himself and the shopkeeper Verloc whose stock in trade in his "ostensible business" is the set of representations in images and texts that do little to stimulate, yet Conrad makes us aware that, unlike Verloc's poor merchandise, Conrad knows how to use his representations to make an outrage hit home brutally (xiv, 3).

The Secret Agent opens in this family shop about which the owner is not very particular, since it is only a front for Verloc's more lucrative political business:

> The window contained photographs of more or less undressed dancing girls; nondescript packages in wrappers like patent medicines; closed yellow paper envelopes, very flimsy, and marked two-and-six in heavy black figures; a few numbers of ancient French comic publications hung across a string as if to dry; a dingy blue china bowl, a casket of black wood, bottles of marking ink, and rubber stamps; a few books, with titles hinting of impropriety; a few apparently old copies of obscure newspapers, badly printed, with titles like *The Torch*, *The Gong*—rousing titles. And the two gas jets inside the panes were always turned low, either for economy's sake or for the sake of the customers. (3–4)

This catalogue of items in the shop window represents the shop's merchandise as haphazard and unattractively packaged with prices printed in heavy ink, the shop wares interspersed in the low-lit window with writing supplies, and a bowl—assorted junk with those suspended "comic publications" hanging makeshift above (3). Such wares, "prophylactics and indecent photographs" as Stephen Donovan remarks, are directed at a male customer, apparently one who lacks the affluence and discrimination to purchase better-quality erotic materials elsewhere—and sometimes the confidence to purchase them there when confronted by Winnie Verloc's impassive gaze at the cash register (Donovan 2005, 148; *SA* 5). The presence of Winnie at the register, despite her youth, attractive figure, and "tight bodice," actually obstructs purchases at the store: "Steady-eyed like her husband, she preserved an air of unfathomable indifference behind the rampart of the counter" (5). Certainly, such reserve might be natural when a "respectable" woman like Winnie prefers not to charm or even engage customers in her pornography shop, and she is reserved in all areas of her life (274). Yet the extent to which the Verlocs are complacent in their financial security and disinterested in selling their wares in the shop is remarkable; their stances counterpoint those scenes where they have to enter the commercial world to represent themselves with high stakes.[2] The fact that Verloc cannot persuade Vladimir of his value as an agent is underscored by painful conversational attempts to justify Verloc's continued relevance to the scornful Vladimir (attempts that, of course, culminate in the bombing), and Winnie's attempt to offer herself to Ossipon sexually to secure him as a protector after Verloc's murder fails notably. After all, the narrative implies, as the novel begins, that the shop itself has already been superseded by urban renewal, located as it is in one of the "grimy brick houses which existed in large quantities before the era of reconstruction dawned upon London" (3).

If Winnie does not associate herself as a woman with any of the erotic images that Verloc purchases abroad for sale in the shop (she appears to find them neither stimulating nor disturbing, though, given the description of the contents of the shop, perhaps that is not surprising), the novel makes clear that she considers sex to be a regular part of her domestic arrangement with Verloc and elliptically gives us Winnie's sexual history. We know that the self-centered Verloc, notably lacking in physical attractiveness, also lacks sympathy for and comprehension of Winnie's emotions and desires with regard to Stevie and Verloc himself. Winnie seems to derive satisfaction from Verloc's desire for her and from fulfilling the role of an "experienced wife," but there is no indication that Winnie has ever felt for Verloc the kind of strong physical attraction that she feels for Ossipon (57). Throughout the novel, Winnie functions as a recognizable version of the Victorian domestic angel, anticipating Verloc's wants for alimentary refreshment and domestic comfort as well as sex. When Verloc returns from his inciting meeting with Vladimir giddy and unwell, "Mrs. Verloc, with all of the placidity of an experienced wife, expressed a confident opinion as to the cause, and suggested the usual remedies; but her husband, rooted in the middle of the room,

---

[2]When Verloc returns from his meeting with Vladimir, he briefly takes stock of the till. The narrator notes that the coins in the till "were but few; and for the first time since he opened his shop he took a commercial survey of its value. The survey was unfavorable. He had gone into trade for no commercial reasons" (54).

shook his lowered head sadly" (57). It is no surprise that, after the disheart-
ening and emasculating meeting with Vladimir, Verloc might not be in the
mood for sex; yet Winnie's "placidity" and "confidence" mark her security
in her marriage and the services she renders. Conrad's deliberate rendering of Winnie's self-sacrifice and the satisfaction it entails on her part evoke
deliberately the nineteenth-century bourgeois values with which she was
raised and upon which she stakes her wifely role. In *The Women of England,
Their Social Duties and Domestic Habits* (1838), that well-known author
of Victorian women's manuals, Sarah Stickney Ellis, emphasizes the patriotic value of a wife skilled in providing the "minutiæ of domestic comfort,"
anticipating her husband's wants and even his conversational preferences
with unobtrusive competence.[3] According to the narrator, Winnie's "wifely
attentions" have been hitherto successful: Verloc "was thoroughly domes-
ticated. Neither his spiritual, nor his mental, nor his physical needs were of
the kind to take him much abroad. He found at home the ease of his body
and the peace of his conscience, together with Mrs Verloc's wifely attentions
and Mrs Verloc's mother's deferential regard" (5–6). The narrator notes
of Winnie, "She did not look for courtesies from him. But he was a good
husband, and she had a loyal respect for his rights" (190–191). Foreseeing
one's husband's needs and supplying his domestic—and, by implication,
erotic—comforts was meant to ensure better morals in men and the kind of
domestic satisfaction that keeps the home intact. Conrad's ironic treatment
of this ideal in Stevie's death and Verloc's murder highlights the false basis
for such domestic ideals; the lack of understanding or communication in the
Verloc household is so complete that neither Winnie nor Verloc perceives
how the other comprehends the basis for their marriage.

It is notable that the Verlocs do not have children of their own,
since a fruitful union is one of the Victorian markers of an appropriate

---

[3] Sarah Stickney Ellis's (1838) inspirational instructions for nineteenth-century domestic
women capture the elevated values that inform Winnie's marital practice:

The women of England, possessing the grand privilege of being better instructed
than those of any other country, in the minutiæ of domestic comfort, have obtained
a degree of importance in society far beyond what their unobtrusive virtues would
appear to claim. The long-established customs of their country have placed in their
hands the high and holy duty of cherishing and protecting the minor morals of life,
from whence springs all that is elevated in purpose, and glorious in action (57).

marriage. Stevie can only serve as an emotional surrogate for a child to Winnie, who grew up as his protector, since Verloc cannot see the value in Stevie, even empathetically through Winnie's eyes. Jeremy Hawthorn (2007) questions whether the Verlocs' lack of a child connects with "a motif of sterility in the novel" (110). Though the Verlocs clearly have a sexual relationship, "[t]he text of the serial edition of the novel makes it absolutely clear that Verloc's shop sells contraceptives in addition to pornography, both of which are associated with forms of sex that do not produce children" (Hawthorn 2007, 110).[4] Like her mother, who fears taxing Mr. Verloc's generosity toward Stevie by remaining as a dependent in Verloc's household, Winnie might want to avoid having a child of her own to ensure Verloc's continued interest in Stevie. Using contraception and, thus, preventing Verloc from fathering a child with her might facilitate the development of a more deeply felt familial relationship between Verloc and Stevie. However, Winnie, "[c]onfident of the power of her charms" is secure of her desirability in Verloc's eyes (190). If Winnie is in a position to influence decisions about contraception, then it might also be that she does not extend their marital bargain to children; she will take care of Verloc's domestic comfort in exchange for Stevie's security, but she cares to offer no further service to Verloc in superintending a larger family.[5]

Certainly, Winnie's loyalty to and concern for Stevie has been the primary consideration in her romantic relationships. Winnie's mother recalls Winnie's promising young romance with the butcher's son, a relationship that ended just as Winnie's mother, concerned about the implications for Stevie's future, feared hearing of the young couple's engagement. After Stevie's death, Winnie's recollections of her practical bargain with Verloc superseding the heartfelt desires of her first love make the extent of her sacrifice clear:

> But this vision had a breath of a hot London summer in it, and for a central figure a young man wearing his Sunday best, with a straw hat on his

---

[4]Hawthorne (2007) continues, "Moreover, early on in the novel the words 'hygiene' and 'protection'—both standard contemporary euphemisms for contraception—are linked decisively with Verloc" (110).

[5]Notably, in Conrad's early story "The Idiots," which I address in the previous chapter, a wife kills her husband as a kind of murderous contraception, when he threatens to rape her to conceive more children.

dark head and a wooden pipe in his mouth. Affectionate and jolly, he was a fascinating companion for a voyage down the sparkling stream of life; only his boat was very small. There was room in it for a girl-partner at the oar, but no accommodation for passengers. He was allowed to drift away from the threshold of the Belgravian mansion while Winnie averted her tearful eyes. He was not a lodger. The lodger was Mr Verloc, indolent, and keeping late hours, sleepily jocular of a morning from under his bed-clothes, but with gleams of infatuation in his heavy lidded eyes, and always with some money in his pockets. There was no sparkle of any kind on the lazy stream of his life. It flowed through secret places. But his barque seemed a roomy craft, and his taciturn magnanimity accepted as a matter of course the presence of passengers. (243)

This description of Winnie's first love uses the metaphor of the shared voyage to create a powerful pictorial image in keeping with Impressionist paintings of such excursions; the notion of an "affectionate and jolly" partner in a "sparkling" vision of Winnie's life clearly is tinged with nostalgia for Winnie's innocence and her past self.[6] In comparison, despite his "gleams of infatuation," Verloc is "taciturn" and "indolent;" his nocturnal habits and "heavy lidded eyes" recall the Darwinian frame of reference that pervades the novel. Until Stevie's death, Winnie feels confident that she has chosen the right man, one who can serve as a more appropriate father figure for Stevie than their own abusive father: "And with peaceful pride she congratulated herself on a certain resolution she had taken a few years before. It had cost her some effort, and even a few tears" (187). As Hawthorn (2007) notes, Winnie "has split sex off from love. Sex with her husband, love with her brother" (112). Yet Winnie's dearly bought sacrifice costs Stevie his life, creating consequences she could have never anticipated. Even as Winnie describes her marriage with Verloc to Ossipon late in the novel, she recalls the sacrifice of her first

---

[6] In *Joseph Conrad and Popular Culture* (2005), Stephen Donovan notes these contexts for Winnie's "vision":

These recollections are heavily inflected with the idiom and visual iconography of popular sentiment: that Winnie's sweetheart is a butcher's son recalls the American ballad 'My True Love is a Butcher's Boy'; and her fantasy of sharing a boat trip [...] evokes the ditty "Row, row, row your boat/Gently down the stream/Merrily, merrily, merrily, merrily/Life is but a dream" as well as the mawkish watercolor on Alvin Hervey's wall in [Conrad's 1898 short story] "The Return" (35).

love for the apparent security Verloc offered: "The memory of the early romance with the young butcher survived, tenacious, like the image of a glimpsed ideal in that heart quailing before the fear of the gallows and full of revolt against death" (243). The loss of this idealized passion continues to call up her outrage even after she has murdered Verloc.

Notably, it is Verloc's demand for sex that seems to lead immediately to his death. When Verloc first mentions fleeing the country with Winnie before she is aware that Stevie is dead, she confidently plays the role of the sexually experienced wife, one who can use her desirability to control her husband:

> She turned her head over her shoulder and gave that man planted heavily in front of the fireplace a glance, half arch, half cruel, out of her large eyes—a glance of which the Winnie of the Belgravian mansion days would have been incapable, because of her respectability and her ignorance. But the man was her husband now, and she was no longer ignorant. She kept it on him for a whole second, with her grave face motionless like a mask, while she said playfully:

> "You couldn't. You would miss me too much." (196)

Normally impassive and expressionless, Winnie performs for her husband using a calculated expression and staged gestures, which she dramatically delays. This moment of playfulness seems to be virtually unique in the descriptions of the Verloc marriage; yet, this moment is also telling, giving the reader insight into Winnie's sense of her own maturation and her security in her marriage. Despite Verloc's limitations, Winnie takes pleasure in her own desirability and in satisfying her husband; however, disturbingly, this scene takes place when Verloc is aware of Stevie's death, but Winnie is not, which lends her performance more poignancy for the reader.

Throughout Winnie and Verloc's interactions immediately preceding his murder, the narration makes much of Verloc's self-centered mindset as he blames Winnie for labeling Stevie (and thus allowing his remains to be identified) and Stevie for blowing himself up, deflecting blame from himself and eventually longing for Winnie to fall into the supportive role of the domestic angel: "But this was not an ordinary evening. It was an occasion when a man wants to be fortified and strengthened by open proofs of sympathy and affection" (252). The tone of the narration here highlights gender roles as "a man" requires his wife to fall into her proper domestic role, supporting her husband and anticipating his needs. The narrator makes it clear that Verloc has not realized that Winnie blames him for Stevie's death and does not comprehend that Stevie's death alters the basis for their marriage in Winnie's eyes. Verloc gets little response from Winnie to all of his complaints and entreaties until he calls to her "with an accent of marital authority": "'Come here,' he said in a peculiar tone, which might have been the tone of brutality, but was intimately known to Mrs Verloc as the note of wooing" (262). The description makes the connection between brutality and sex with the ironic use of the courtly term "wooing"; Winnie may have been wooed by the butcher's son, especially in her nostalgic vision of him, but Verloc has never made much special effort for Winnie, accepting her affection as his due. He takes Winnie for granted in her domestic duties, including her sexual ministrations, and it is his call for sex that causes her to advance towards him, seemingly obedient as she picks up the knife. That "[h]e would want to keep her for nothing" was Winnie's fear (256). Conrad portrays her fear in starkly economic terms, illuminating Winnie's rejection of the wifely role she has hitherto embraced, albeit with reservations. Throughout these scenes, Conrad is in dialog with Victorian conventions about gender and marriage, ironically highlighting the absurd and oppressive expectations about women and sexuality that structure Winnie's marriage. In a sense, Conrad acknowledges that the shop's pornography with its faded pictures of staged dancers represents the faded bourgeois attitudes about marital submission that form the basis for the Verlocs' union, which emphasizes those conventionalized roles. Winnie is fully honest and direct with Verloc only when she wields the carving knife.

II

Winnie's atavistic regression before the murder can be linked ironically to her liberation from her marital contract by Stevie's death. The theme of degeneration pervades the novel, which frames it as pervasive in the world of the text, and the discredited science of Lombroso's criminal anthropology becomes another kind of pornography in Conrad's rendering. Ossipon, the "ex-medical student without a degree," makes reference to contemporary criminologist Cesare Lombroso by name early in the novel when he superciliously categorizes Stevie as a degenerate (46–47).[7] Conrad undercuts Ossipon's authority and sets the tone for the novel's use of Lombrosian taxonomies by describing Ossipon in terms which make Ossipon himself a degenerate according to Lombroso's racist classifications: "A bush of crinkly yellow hair topped his red, freckled face, with a flattened nose and prominent mouth cast in the rough mould of the negro type" (44).[8] Conrad effectively mimics and adapts Lombroso's tone, implying that Lombroso's resonant images of criminals and anatomizing descriptions of their bodies would be equally at home in the Verlocs' pornography shop, which attracts degenerate consumers and degenerate anarchists alike. Notably, Lombroso's quasi-scientific tomes use photographs of criminals and prostitutes (recalling the shop's "faded, yellow dancing girls") alongside evocative descriptions and intriguing anecdotal narratives: he writes, "Still more typically homicidal and lascivious, in my opinion is the female criminal Berland. Here we have sunken eyes, a receding forehead, a small head, sessile ears, [...] and a virile physiognomy" (Lombroso and Ferraro 1915, 96).[9] In *The Female Offender*, Lombroso helpfully comments on the women's relative attractiveness ("quite pretty" and "justly celebrated for their beauty") along with their other notable traits (100). Lombroso's classifications extend and offer further scientific legitimacy

---

[7] Conrad's precise familiarity with Lombroso is unclear, but *The Female Offender* (1915) (written with his assistant Guglielmo Ferrero) appeared in English translation in 1895, *Crime: Its Causes and Remedies* in English 1899, and his daughter Gina Lombroso Ferraro's well-known distillation of her father's ideas in *Criminal Man* was translated only in 1911.

[8] To underscore this ironic treatment of Lombroso, the irascible anarchist Karl Yundt memorably intones in response to Ossipon's reverent allusion to Lombroso, "Lombroso is an ass" (*SA* 77).

[9] For example, the 1915 edition of Lombroso and Ferraro's *The Female Offender* "specially published" in New York for the Brunswick Subscription Company contains a significant number photographs of women meant to signify in one instance the "Physiognomy of Russian Female Offenders" in a chapter on "Facial and Cephalic Anomalies of Female Criminals." The images are interspersed with cranial measurements and discussion of various anatomical anomalies: "*Projecting cheek-bones.*—Found among 19 per cent of criminals, especially murderesses (30 per cent), among 40 per cent of prostitutes, and 14 per cent of normals. (*See* Plate I., 3, 7, 9, 15, 20; Plate II., 2, 3, 4, 6, 7, 8, 16, 17, 23.)" (77). Though presented as a scientific study, such images of criminals clearly invite a salacious gaze, Lombroso's scientific pretentions excusing an appraising inventory of their degenerate bodies. Perhaps especially appealing to the subscribers, Lombroso includes three full-page photographs of Charlotte Corday's skull in this volume.

to Victorian gender hierarchies that idealize women's purity and the avoidance of strong passions in women. In Conrad's study of Winnie, he might be said to enlarge upon such problematic capsule narratives of female criminals, infusing the gothic imaginary of the Victorian sensation novel with the popular criminological perspective of the phrenologist. Conrad implicitly critiques the pornographic nature of Lombroso's eroticized appraisals of women's degenerate bodies.

In *Decadent Subjects* Charles Bernheimer (2002), considers Lombroso's influence at the *fin de siècle*: "The project of cataloguing ever more degenerates in order to manage their exclusion from a healthy body politic risks overwhelming a shrinking center of normalcy by an expanding margin of deviance" (142). One might read *The Secret Agent* as establishing this "center of normalcy" as a fiction, as it expands the "margin of deviance" to encompass so many of the novel's characters, whom it portrays as subject to their instincts and desires, able to give only lip service to any abstract notion of good. By, in effect, refuting Lombroso's binaries, which subordinate and pathologize a subset of the population, Conrad insists that self-interest and corruption are not the province of deviant criminals with marked bodies, but are intrinsic to the nature of our common humanity.

While Winnie's love for Stevie appears to be altruistic, Conrad also presents it as self-interested in that Winnie uses her commitment to Stevie as the touchstone for her existence, the role that gives her life meaning. When Mrs. Verloc comes upon the unwary Verloc to kill him, the narrative describes her gradual degeneration: "Mrs Verloc was coming. As if the homeless soul of Stevie had flown for shelter straight to the breast of his sister, guardian and protector, the resemblance of her face with that of her brother grew at every step, even to the droop of the lower lip, even to the slight divergence of the eyes. But Mr Verloc did not see that" (262). In Conrad's ironic method, he uses the very Lombrosian taxonomies debunked elsewhere in the novel to frame Winnie's "murdering mad" blow into which she "had put all the inheritance of her immemorial and obscure descent, the simple ferocity of the age of caverns, and the unbalanced nervous fury of the age of bar-rooms" (263). Conrad's depiction of Winnie's violence recalls Lombroso's theories about "maternal passion,"[10] as she degenerates,

---

[10]For more information on this connection, see the previous chapter and my article, "The Female Offender, the New Woman, and Winnie Verloc in Conrad's *The Secret Agent*" (Harrington 2007).

reproducing Stevie's visage in her own as she takes primitive revenge for his untimely death: Bernheimer explains, "Anatomy reveals itself to Lombroso as destiny, a retrograde destiny in the case of the criminal, who reproduces in the present a primitive stage of evolution that is now anomalous, even monstrous" (142). Conrad signals a similar understanding of Lombroso to Bernheimer, in recalling Winnie's "descent" from "the age of caverns" and "the age of bar-rooms" as though centuries of inherited violence are unleashed into contemporary London from her once peaceable form (263).

The other significant context for Winnie's degeneracy and the murder of Verloc is women's liberation: Conrad makes it clear that, without Stevie, the Verlocs have no marriage agreement, since their marriage was, unbeknownst to Verloc, contingent on Stevie's security and well-being. By highlighting the transactional nature of the Verlocs' marriage in Winnie's eyes, Conrad invites a critique of the women's limited choices in the Victorian period. Winnie can choose between men to facilitate the best possible life for her and her brother, but beyond that she can only perform her domestic duties impeccably:

> Mrs. Verloc pursued the visions of seven years' security for Stevie, loyally paid for on her part; of security growing into confidence, into a domestic feeling, stagnant and deep like a placid pool, whose guarded surface hardly shuddered on the occasional passage of Comrade Ossipon, the robust anarchist with shamelessly inviting eyes, whose glance had a corrupt clearness sufficient to enlighten any woman not absolutely imbecile. (243)

By describing her familial feeling as "stagnant and deep," Conrad emphasizes the extent to which Winnie's relationship with Verloc and their mutual understanding remain unchanged and undeveloped, as though she must avert her eyes to perpetuate it. Winnie uses her commitment to her family to push aside the sexual attraction she feels for the leering Ossipon, the shudder on that surface of the metaphorical pool indicating that her erotic feeling is not repressed fully. Ossipon uses his relationships with a series of women to finance his leisure, avoiding the kind of domestic commitments that his fellow anarchist Verloc made in marrying Winnie, and his "shamelessly" direct admiration of Winnie seems to be unique for her in the retired life she leads. She has previously avoided mentioning Ossipon to Verloc as one of the series of visitors

who called in Verloc's absence abroad.[11] Out of discretion as well as loyalty to Verloc, Winnie will not mention Ossipon or betray her attraction
for him with more than "the faintest possible blush"; doing anything
more than repressing her consciousness of an attraction to another man
might invite her to acknowledge the extent of her dissatisfaction in her
marriage (183). It is hardly surprising that a marriage undertaken merely
to secure Stevie's continued well-being might not be particularly personally or sexually fulfilling, and Winnie knows she must take pleasure in the
proper performance of her contractual role than through the pursuit of
her own desires. Winnie's attraction to Ossipon runs through the novel
and foreshadows her attempt at a bargain with him at the end of the
novel.

After Verloc's death, the newly-liberated Winnie, the "free woman,"
finds herself unable to conceive of a life outside of her existence as a
wife and quasi-mother to Stevie: "It came to her suddenly. Murderers
escaped. They escaped abroad. Spain or California. Mere names" (270).
Conrad here highlights the ways that Winnie's consumption of popular crime narratives (those "illustrative woodcuts to a certain type of
tales")[12] and newspaper accounts influences her behavior. Winnie is pro-
foundly fearful of the gallows as the penalty for her crime, and so she
quickly reverts to the submissive feminine role into which she has been
socialized as powerfully as her innate fear of execution for crime. Coming
upon Ossipon who is "skulking" in a cowardly fashion in the street with
designs on Winnie's money, Winnie immediately seeks Ossipon as a
protector; she envisions him as "a radiant messenger of life," the savior
image suffused with her once suppressed erotic feeling for him (274).

---

[11] "Of Comrade Ossipon, whom she had received curtly, entrenched behind the counter
with a stony face and a faraway gaze, she said nothing, her mental reference to the robust
anarchist being marked by a short pause, with the faintest possible blush" (183); "Mrs
Verloc declared her affection for Michaelis; mentioned her abhorrence of Karl Yundt, 'nasty
old man'; and of Ossipon she said nothing" (189).

[12] Winnie may be referring to the familiar and inexpensive broadsheet ballads embellished
with woodcuts that were sold during the brief interval between sentencing and execution
or to an illustrated morality tale: according to Donovan (2005), "Whether a memory of
Thomas Bewick's often-reproduced 'Gibbet' of 1821 or, as seems more probably, an illustration from a mid-century morality tale, Winnie's woodcut attests to the simple power of
monochrome shading and simple design to evoke a condemned criminal's end. The popularity of even crude broadside woodcuts [...] lasted well into the second half of the nineteenth century" (41).

Once Ossipon realizes that Winnie has murdered her husband, Ossipon becomes "terrified scientifically," since, as the narrator notes, he "was free from the trammels of conventional morality—but he submitted to the rule of science" (290, 297). Vladimir has already referred to science as the "sacrosanct fetish" of the day (33), but here Conrad masterfully demonstrates this through Ossipon's attempt to apply Lombroso's principles to Winnie, infusing the fateful scene with striking comedy:

> He was scientific, and he gazed scientifically at that woman, the sister of a degenerate, a degenerate herself—of a murdering type. He gazed at her, and invoked Lombroso, as an Italian peasant recommends himself to his favourite saint. He gazed scientifically. He gazed at her cheeks, at her nose, at her eyes, at her ears. ... Bad! ... Fatal! Mrs Verloc's pale lips parting, slightly relaxed under his passionately attentive gaze, he gazed also at her teeth. ... Not a doubt remained ... a murdering type.... (297)

Conrad takes care to have Ossipon apply Lombroso's principles in detail, anatomizing Winnie's features and finding each one confirms her degeneracy, before making the inevitable diagnosis. This parodic representation of Lombroso's principles, as Ossipon uses them to distance himself from Winnie and shore up his own questionable authority, offers a powerful critique of the kind of quasi-scientific certitude phrenology represents, as well as its power to predict morality and define identity through external signs on the body. Conrad makes it clear that Ossipon takes refuge in ideological principles that allow him to disavow his own terror at Winnie's rage and their common humanity and that such principles are based on faith rather than reason, embodying the very religious fervor that Ossipon despises in others.

Ironically, Winnie's death ruins Ossipon; just as her contract with Verloc is nullified by Stevie's death, Ossipon can no longer work for his livelihood and to maintain his ego after her death: "The confiding disposition of various classes of women satisfied the needs of his self-love, and put some material means into his hand. He needed it to live. It was there. But if he could no longer make use of it, he ran the risk of starving his ideals and his body" (307). Conrad makes it clear that Ossipon also had made a career of selling himself for financial security, echoing Winnie's pragmatic choice to accept Verloc as her husband instead of the butcher's son (though, in Conrad's broad irony, Winnie has, in a sense married the butcher), even as he construed women as goods, a replaceable series of generous and admiring marks for his manipulation, offering money, sex, and adulation to the ex-medical student.

By the end of the novel, Ossipon has accepted the cruelty of his actions and cannot live with himself without drinking heavily. When the Professor goads him, "Tell me, Ossipon, terrible man, has ever one of your victims killed herself for you—or are your triumphs so far incomplete—for blood alone puts a seal on greatness? Blood. Death. Look at history," Ossipon cannot revel in his strength and the weakness of others (304). Alluding to the tragic image of the female suicide (considered in detail in the next chapter), the Professor evokes another familiar representation of women to mock Ossipon contemptuously, since Ossipon allows himself the weakness of sympathizing with Winnie and being horrified at his role in her death. Ossipon's willingness to use women for financial support—effectively prostituting himself—is well established.[13] Hawthorn (2007) notes the way in which Ossipon's behavior to Winnie recalls Winnie's treatment of Verloc: "Having used the pretense of love to gain Verloc's protection of her brother, she finds that she is treated in the same way by Ossipon, who also promises love and then cruelly abandons her once he has his hands on her money" (111). Such cycles of cruelty reinforce the novel's portrayal of a society lacking in compassion and fellow feeling, one in which the values of the market generally supersede human comradeship.

Conrad emphasizes Winnie's internalization of Victorian marital ideology, as well as her internalization of newspaper accounts of judicial authority, which influence her behavior to an extent of which she seems unaware. Nor can Ossipon get the newspaper account out of his head, since he knows the solution to the "*impenetrable mystery*" of what motivated the lady passenger to commit suicide: "behind that white mask of despair there was struggling against terror and despair a vigour of vitality, a love of life that could resist the furious anguish which drives to murder and the fear, the blind, mad fear of the gallows" (307–308). He can no longer view her as a mark whose money he needs to skillfully maneuver out of her hands, a woman who can flatter his ego and stoke his desire. Ossipon knows the story of Winnie's death, sensing the struggle of her vitality against the instinctual drives to which she is subject, and cannot

---

[13] Early in the novel, Verloc thinks, "As to Ossipon, that beggar was sure to want for nothing as long as there were silly girls with savings-bank books in the world" (53).

live with the horror which he has glimpsed and his role in it. As such, we might take this Ossipon, after Winnie's death, as a kind of figure for the reader, clutching the account of her death and witness to the nihilist conclusions of *The Secret Agent*, which leaves us only with the narcissistic Professor, "unsuspected and deadly, like a pest in the street full of men" (311). By structuring the novel to emphasize the ways in which human beings understand ourselves and each other, not through empathy and enlightened self-knowledge, but by identifying with a series of representations and taxonomies, Conrad shows the shallow and self-gratifying nature of our interactions, the extent to which we are limited by our solipsistic tendencies. In *The Secret Agent*, the characters' altruistic sentiments and adherence to principle are mainly revealed to be pretenses that they use to rationalize the deeper drives that animate them.

Thus, Winnie's early passion to protect Stevie has become the primary drive in her nature. As she mechanically fulfills her traditional womanly duties as wife and quasi-mother, Conrad makes us uncomfortably aware how much, in her circumscribed, traditional role, she serves as the counterpart to the eroticized images of women who appear to represent the very opposite of her dearly bought bourgeois respectability. Though Winnie sees those "faded, yellow dancing girls" only as merchandise for the shop, she, too, has been pressed into service, satisfying Verloc's needs in exchange for security for herself and Stevie (5). She cannot conceive of her own liberty, and she is defined almost entirely through her relationships with men: her father, Stevie, Verloc, and Ossipon. Her reluctance to avoid considering Verloc's behavior and her own situation too closely—"[T]hings do not stand much looking into" (177)—is revealed ironically to be a good coping strategy, since, when Winnie is forced to consider her husband's nature and the nature of their marriage more closely, she murders Verloc and eventually commits suicide. There are obviously no good alternatives for Winnie before or after Verloc's demise, but nonetheless Conrad acknowledges that her role is untenable.

III

While *Victory* does not focus on pornography or eroticized images of women, the novel does consider how we look at women as it stages them repeatedly for evaluative male audiences in different contexts, continually making women subject to a discerning male eye. Conrad's deliberate rendering of these women, in particular Lena and Mrs. Schomberg, who struggle to navigate an existence in which they are subject to men's desires and assumptions, revisits the critique of women as goods, objects in a sexual marketplace that serves men. Through the character of Lena, the novel also invites us to consider how women are influenced by familiar representations and expectations as they try to envision and fulfill women's roles in a changing cultural context.

In a sense, Conrad (2016) initially sets up Lena, whom Schomberg desires as his mistress, and Mrs. Schomberg, Schomberg's brutalized wife, as exhibits, and the descriptions of Mrs. Schomberg in particular might recall Conrad's ironic rendering of Lombroso's case studies in *The Secret Agent*. Though Mrs. Schomberg is not a criminal, Conrad 2016 treats her as a psychological study whose "wooden" demeanor gradually reveals unexpected depths to Davidson (46). When he first enters Schomberg's hotel, Davidson notes the concert posters on the walls surrounding him: "A poster of "Concerts Every Evening," like those on the gate, but in a good state of preservation, hung on the wall fronting him. He looked at it idly and was struck by the fact (then not so very common) that it was a ladies' orchestra. 'Zangiacomo's Eastern Tour. Eighteen Performers" (45). The poster makes it a selling point that the women of the orchestra have played before not just the European men of the colonial administration, but "Pashas, Sheiks, Chiefs," and a sultan; as such, they form a kind of exhibit of European woman on a colonial tour, showcasing their—apparently quite limited—musical skills for local and colonial officials (45). Based solely on reading the poster, Davidson immediately feels sympathy for the women of the orchestra, musing on their plight: "Davidson felt sorry for the eighteen lady-performers. He knew what that sort of life was like, the sordid conditions and brutal incidents of such tours led by such Zangiacomos" (45). Of course, all kinds of female performers at this time might be presumed to be sexually available as lovers or prostitutes, and the combination of the adjectives "sordid" and "brutal" seems to link sex and violence with the poverty and disenfranchisement of these women. Hawthorn (2007) argues, "Conrad's presentation of the Ladies Orchestra makes it clear that there is a sort of sexual commerce involved in the performance that situates prostitution at the centre of the cultural exchange depicted in the novel, not on its margins" (126). Indeed, the reader is invited to make the connection between the erotic availability represented by the purchased, staged performance itself and the sexual commerce to which such a performance might lead; perhaps his is why Schomberg insists that the orchestra members must circulate in the audience, cadging drinks and gauging interest.

Davidson's musing on the orchestra is immediately interrupted by another kind of live exhibit, Mrs. Schomberg, whom he later compares to an "automaton" (46):

> While he was staring at the poster, a door somewhere at his back opened, and a woman came in who was looked upon as Schomberg's wife, no doubt with truth. As somebody remarked cynically once, she was too unattractive to be anything else. The opinion that he treated her abominably was based on her frightened expression. Davidson lifted his hat to her.

> Mrs. Schomberg gave him an inclination of her sallow head and incontinently sat down behind a sort of raised counter facing the door with a mirror and rows of bottles at her back. (45)

Of necessity, Mrs. Schomberg cultivates a rigid impassivity that Davidson characterizes as so striking as to be almost absurd, the result of years of abuse by her husband. With her silk gown and wooden demeanor, Mrs. Schomberg acts as a kind of parody of idealized Victorian womanhood, her absurd formality complemented by her wretched submission. She clings to her abuser, and the only glimpses of initiative and mental acuity on her part evident to the reader are the actions she takes as part of the conspiracy to help Heyst "steal" Lena, when she shows cunning and engagement that are utterly at odds with her cultivated immobility (78). Ironically, Conrad indicates that Mrs. Schomberg participates in the conspiracy, a kind of wifely revolt on her part, in order to preserve her horrible marriage, since she has no other options but to stay with Schomberg. Like Winnie, who, even after Verloc betrays her and she murders him, cannot envision a life for herself other than one in which she subordinates herself to a dominant man, Mrs. Schomberg cannot be liberated from the pervasive scripts about gender that rule her behavior.

Of course, Mrs. Schomberg also serves as a cautionary story for Lena, who recognizes the vulnerability in her own abject position and the extent to which both Schomberg's wife and Zangiacomo's performers must prostitute themselves in order to survive. As the youthful erotic prize in a matronly orchestra, Lena represents a better class of goods to be sold or leveraged as Zangiacomo sees fit. Lena's father, immobilized by a stroke and lodged at a far remove at a home for "incurables," cannot offer her protection or support, so her employment with Zangiacomo offers her occupation and the pretense of respectability (77). While Lena's decision to flee with the gentle and compassionate Heyst is understandable given these conditions, Davidson longs to understand why Heyst has fled with her: "When you say an English girl, Mrs. Schomberg, do you really mean a young girl? Some of these orchestra girls are no chicks," which is, of course, true of Lena's older fellow performers (40–41). Later, he comments, "I imagine the girl must have been specially attractive," but Mrs. Schomberg responds only that she is "miserable" with few possessions to pack: "I don't suppose it was more than a little linen and a couple of those white frocks they wear on the platform" (50). Mrs. Schomberg can only reply with regard to the paucity of possessions she helped bundle in her shawl, but Davidson and the narrator who is his interlocutor are trying to judge her value on the market—and so understand Heyst's motivations by matching them to a common, comprehensible narrative of his desire for a beautiful young woman: "It was really provoking that Davidson should not be able to give one some idea of the girl. Was she pretty? He didn't know" (61). Like the narrator, Davidson, too, is curious enough to change his habits to solicit information about Lena in particular:

> His proceeding was to enter into conversation with one and another, casually, and showing no particular knowledge of the affair, in order to discover something about the girl. Was she anything out of the way? Was she pretty?
>
> She couldn't have been markedly so. She had not attracted special notice. She was young. On that everybody agreed. The English clerk of Tesmans' remembered that she had a sallow face. He was respectable and highly proper. He was not the sort to associate with such people. Most of these women were fairly battered specimens. (61)

Perhaps Davidson is using his curiosity to fill time between voyages, but he seems particularly concerned with other European men's valuation of Lena's worth in beauty.

The consensus seems to be that, while young, Lena must not be beautiful enough to have attracted "special notice," especially with her sallow complexion[14]; it is Lena's youth and relative freshness compared to the other "battered specimens" that make up the women's orchestra that make her a commodity. Given what we know about Schomberg's abuse of his wife, Conrad has chosen the term "battered" to highlight the extent to which these women, as wives and in the orchestra, are treated as goods to be assessed, possessed, and potentially abused, and "specimen" recalls the appraising scientific or commercial eye with which they are viewed. As Heyst's offer to Lena to steal her makes clear, they are both aware that she is a commodity, especially given her unspent youth, which the narrative contrasts powerfully with Mrs. Schomberg's aged and abused form: Schomberg "never glanced her way, for the reason that Mrs. Schomberg in her night attire looked the most unattractive object in existence, miserable, insignificant, faded, crushed, old. And the contrast with the feminine form he had ever in his mind's eye made his wife's appearance painful to his esthetic sense" (98). The narrator makes it clear that Mrs. Schomberg cannot charm her husband even in the more forgiving half-light at bedtime; he has the barely suppressed desire to harm her mortally, since she represents his marital commitment, his age, and the cumulative effects of his abuse of her, but, in contrast, his erotic imagination has been captured by Lena, especially in his fantasies of invigorating sex with her. This seems to imply that, not only does Schomberg reject his wife sexually, he views her as a sign of his own aging and a responsibility that depletes him. Mrs. Schomberg's presumed fears are accurate, as Schomberg makes it clear to Lena that he considers his wife expendable and sees Lena as her replacement: "'We'll soon get rid of the old woman,' he whispered to her hurriedly, with panting ferocity. 'Hang her! I've never cared for her. The climate don't suit her; I shall tell her to go to her people in Europe. She will have to go, too! I will see to it'" (90). As he attempts to conspire with Lena, Schomberg openly portrays his wife as unwanted goods, which he has a right to return at will and replace with another model.

The narrator notes that Schomberg is also aware of the distinct advantage he has over Lena: "For he had little doubt of his personal fascination and still less of his power to get hold of that girl worse than friendless, since she had incurred for some reason the animosity of Mrs. Zangiacomo (who had no conscience) and seemed too ignorant to know

---

[14]Notably, Mrs. Schomberg's complexion is also described as "sallow" (45).

how to help herself" (89). Schomberg has such confidence in his situation and his "personal fascination" set against Lena's weak (friendless, "ignorant") position that he is able to disregard her carefully expressed aversion: "The aversion she showed him as far as she dared (for it is not always safe for the helpless to display the delicacy of their sentiments), Schomberg pardoned on the score of feminine conventional silliness" (89–90). By attributing this attitude to Schomberg, Conrad is able to invite criticism of Schomberg's thoughtless and self-serving misogyny; he thinks so little of Lena's humanity that he cannot imagine her having a different preference as anything but "silliness," which seems to imply that she must be a woman who does not know her own mind or one who chooses to misrepresent her position. In so "pardoning" her, Schomberg neatly dismisses Lena's ability to choose for herself; he longs to maneuver her so strategically that her acquiescence is an afterthought. Yet, as she expresses to Heyst, Lena is powerfully aware of Schomberg's machinations and how they objectify both Mrs. Schomberg and herself. She identifies Mrs. Schomberg's disquiet and characterizes their situation quite succinctly: "Another one that can't sleep o' nights. Why? Don't you see why? Because of me, of course. Don't you think she sees what's going on? That beast doesn't even try to keep it from her very much. If she had only the least bit of spirit! She knows how I feel too, only she's too frightened even to look him in the face let alone open her mouth. He would tell her to go hang herself" (83). Confronted with her own lack of options, Lena can identify easily Mrs. Schomberg's circumscribed role and the lack of "spirit," which is probably the result of so many years of Schomberg's abuse and her attempts to avoid his beatings. While the two women do not appear to commiserate, each is able to understand the other's dispossessed position from the vantage point of her own situation, and they work together to frustrate Schomberg's scheme in a way that suits them both.

Even as he struggles to assess Lena's value, the "sensitive" Davidson has already realized her plight: "The girl must have been miserable indeed to follow a strange man to such a spot" (48). Peter Lancelot Mallios (2003) notes the ways in which Conrad inflects familiar archetypes with deeper psychological importance: "The familiar convention of a damsel in distress becomes a disturbing occasion on which to consider a hopelessness (Lena's) bordering on suicide" (170). Given her situation, Lena, who is not yet twenty, can only choose between two middle-aged men: Schomberg in his brutal amorousness, as he longs to use her to regain his manhood; and Heyst in his detached compassion tinged with growing desire for her. Later in the novel, when Ricardo attempts to rape Lena on the island, the reader might view his violence as a crude extension of the male prerogative implied in Schomberg's attempted domination of her in which she is valued only as a desirable object, able to provide gratification to an aggressive man who can possess her. When Lena fights off Ricardo powerfully and silently, his valuation of her changes immediately, and he starts to see her as someone of hidden attractions beyond her physical presence, a worthy and desirable partner or co-conspirator. But Heyst's ambivalence about Lena persists until her death.

Throughout his hurried courtship of Lena, Heyst finds himself enthralled by her and suspicious of her femininity, which he associates with seductive deception that might corrupt his individuality. When he orders Lena to fake a smile to put Schomberg off the track of their conspiracy, Heyst is struck by the effect: "the effect of the mechanical, ordered smile was joyous, radiant. It astonished Heyst. No wonder, it flashed through his mind, women can deceive men so completely. The faculty was inherent in them; they seemed to be created with a special aptitude" (79). Though Heyst has been inspired to assist Lena by the same characteristic compassion that inspired him to assist Morrison, he fears that his instinctive reaction to her femininity, which he defines as threateningly distinct from his masculinity, makes him prey to his desires and her natural manipulations. The very nature of such a "mechanical" smile recalls both the automaton-like quality of Mrs. Schomberg and the staged performances through which Lena makes her living. Though Heyst asked her to smile, he distrusts her success in delivering a smile on demand and the effects it has on him: "Here was a smile the origin of which was well known to him; and yet it had conveyed a sensation of warmth, had given him a sort of ardour to live which was very new to his experience" (79). Even as he distrusts her inherent feminine faculty for deception and communicates his reservations to Lena, he finds himself carried away by his desire for her and the pleasure of close companionship. Leslie Heywood observes, "Sexual difference is the most significantly marked opposition in the text, and is articulated through the various terms used to designate Lena" including Magdalen, Lena, Alma, and presumably "whore" in Schomberg's complaint (Heywood 1994, 8–9; *V* 52).

Lena sagely reminds Heyst of the way men react to her: "I know what sort of girl I am. But all the same I am not the sort that men turn their backs on—and you ought to know it" (82). Initially frustrated by Heyst's change of demeanor, which signals his discomfort with competing with other men for her as the rare commodity of a European woman in the archipelago, Lena quickly affirms that she likes Heyst because he is not like other men in his treatment of her. She remains uncertain until he touches her and pulls her to him in compassion as well as desire. It is Lena's remaining uncertainty that seems to move her towards framing a familiar role for herself: if she cannot be the domestic angel, given her sexual past, she can assist Heyst without his knowledge, a self-sacrificing Magdalen purified by her love and eventually by her death. While I discuss Lena's positioning as a fallen woman and its implications in terms of gender and colonialism in the fifth chapter, Lena's adherence to learned gender norms and her internalization of an ideal of feminine self-sacrifice are also relevant here: Robert Hampson (1996) explains, "the narrative shows how, under the influence of her Sunday school lessons and Victorian constructions of femininity, she writes a script for herself in which erotic feelings are displaced into idealistic self-sacrifice" (245). Certainly, Lena's sense of Heyst's intellectual mistrust of his instinct and emotion seem to cause her attempt to assert herself in a familiar sacrificial role, effectively defining a role for him in relation to her that inverts his initial rescue of her. Conrad makes it apparent that both Lena and Heyst are influenced by gender preconceptions that affect their behavior and assumptions about each other, and their lack of communication causes Heyst to become distrustful and Lena to become desperate.

In sacrificing herself in a secret attempt to save Heyst, Lena fulfills his fears about the archetypically conniving women (the natural corollary to a woman's power traditionally being located in her influence over men, as writers like Sarah Stickney Ellis advocated), yet she does so in a selfless way that makes his fears baseless and obligates him to her. For all of his willingness to live hermetically, outside of the constraints of society, and his ability to empathize with Lena—in marked contrast to Schomberg—Heyst cannot see Lena as an equal. His passion for her makes him too vulnerable, so, even as a liberal-minded man, he continues to view her as the desirable and threatening Eve in his Edenic retreat. Though Lena does not commit suicide as Winnie does, the Professor's words to Ossipon in the last scene of *The Secret Agent* illuminate the resolution of *Victory* as well: as noted earlier in this chapter, the Professor asks

Ossipon whether a woman has ever killed herself for him, "—or are your triumphs so far incomplete—for blood alone puts a seal on greatness? Blood. Death. Look at history" (304). But Lena's self-sacrifice inverts the Professor's assumption that self-sacrifice implies status or triumph for the surviving partner. Conrad (2016) ironically locates her bitter triumph as, in some sense, the point of the novel in his 1920 Author's Note to *Victory*: "And in view of her triumphant end what more could I have done for her rehabilitation and her happiness?" (xvii). This implies that Lena is satisfied by the gesture, which is itself a kind of fulfillment that definitively establishes her as the natural opposite of a conniving "whore," redeeming herself by her fidelity in death, an archetypal reformed prostitute as her Magdalen identity suggests. The hollow nature of this victory, that Lena can triumph only by sacrificing herself in service of another patriarchal narrative, establishing an understanding with Heyst only in death, resonates interestingly with the ending of *Lord Jim*, since Jim can be seen to function similarly to Lena—and frustratingly for Marlow—at the behest of romantic convention. Betty Vanderwielen (1994) aptly connects this back to Lena's foundational, familial Victorian conditioning: "In the end, then, Lena has succeeded only in perfecting the lesson she learned as her father's daughter [...]. Operating under a patriarchal ideology, she considers herself preeminently victorious" (209). It is worth noting, however, that Lena's self-sacrifice, betraying Ricardo to prove herself to Heyst, also represents a singular assertion of self against the oppressive sexual market that has defined her primarily in terms of her desirability to men, an interpretation that I will consider more fully in the fifth chapter; if Heyst can save Lena from Schomberg, then she, too, can play the hero, but by leveraging the role of the damsel.

Both *Victory* and *The Secret Agent* consider—to rich effect—the extent to which ingrained narratives about gender framed in part through popular representations inhibit liberty and intimacy, reducing individuals to their associations with familiar plots, representations, and taxonomies which are often portrayed as reductive, inaccurate, or unjust. To return to Mallios's (2003) point about the relationship of art to convention in Conrad's work, "perhaps the surest mark of sincerity in *Victory* lies in the gravity and self-consciousness with which the novel insists upon taking 'popular' conventions and converting them into serious human issues" (170). The novels highlight the dark comedy in our attempts to narrate and categorize human behavior in reductive and self-serving ways, even as *Victory* and *The Secret Agent* acknowledge that such futile attempts are also tragic, resulting in profound miscomprehension and fundamental alienation. Conrad's use of irony in both novels enables him to depict patriarchal structures from within, critiquing them by deploying the very taxonomies and formulaic plots familiar from popular representations. Conrad allows us to observe and sympathize with Lena and Winnie even as he acknowledges the extent to which contemporary British culture and even his own fiction objectifies them.

Notably, both novels take seriously, at times literally, the Victorian anxiety that the economy surrounding marriage and other erotic markets for women results in a disenfranchisement so profound for women that it turns all women into prostitutes, forced to trade sex and domestic service for personal and financial security. Here, Conrad broaches a political critique of traditional presumptions about gender through his use of gendered representations, exposing the ugly underpinnings of the core Victorian familial ideal as he situates the family home behind a pornography shop. Conrad's late novels prove adept, perhaps surprisingly so, at acknowledging the extent to which women's choices are circumscribed by economic and erotic bargains of the sort which cause Winnie to avert her eyes without looking into them and Lena to attempt to script a different role, albeit one that hews to convention. As Lombroso aptly notes, with his characteristic, persuasive confidence, "The primitive woman was rarely a murderess; but she was always a prostitute, and such she remained until semi-civilized epochs" (Lombroso and Ferraro 1915, 111). Conrad's play on Lombrosian categories deftly undermines Lombroso's taxonomies and the patriarchal subjection that they exemplify, allowing Conrad to critique the broader social context through his cutting satire of Lombroso as scientist—and saint. Fittingly for their early twentieth-century milieu, *The Secret Agent* and *Victory* highlight the extent to which contemporary society harkens back to the primitive.

REFERENCES

Bernheimer, Charles. 2002. Decadent Subjects: The Idea of Decadence. In *Art, Literature, Philosophy, and the Culture of the Fin de Siècle in Europe*, ed. T. Jefferson Kline and Naomi Schor. Baltimore: Johns Hopkins University Press.

Conrad, Joseph. 1924a. Author's Note to *The Secret Agent: A Simple Tale*, vii–xv. Garden City: Doubleday, Page, and Company.

———. 1924b. *The Secret Agent: A Simple Tale*. Garden City, NY: Doubleday, Page, and Company.

————. 2016. In *Victory: An Island Tale*, ed. J.H. Stape and Alexandre Fachard. Cambridge: Cambridge University Press.

Donovan, Stephen. 2005. *Joseph Conrad and Popular Culture*. Basingstoke, UK: Palgrave Macmillan.

Ellis, Sarah Stickney. (1838) 1999. The Women of England. In *Victorian Prose*, ed. Rosemary J. Mundhenk and LuAnn McCracken Fletcher, 53–57. New York: Columbia University Press.

Hampson, Robert. 1996. The Late Novels. In *The Cambridge Companion to Joseph Conrad*, ed. J.H. Stape, 140–159. Cambridge: Cambridge University Press.

Harrington, Ellen Burton. 2007. The Female Offender, The New Woman, and Winnie Verloc in *The Secret Agent*. *The Conradian* 32 (1): 57–69.

Hawthorn, Jeremy. 2007. *Sexuality and the Erotic in the Fiction of Joseph Conrad*. London: Continuum.

Heywood, Leslie. 1994. The Unreadable Text: Conrad and 'The Enigma of Woman' in *Victory*. *Conradiana* 26 (1): 3–19.

Lombroso, Caesar and William Ferraro (Lombroso, Cesare and Guglielmo Ferrero). 1915. *The Female Offender*. New York: Appleton and Co.

Mallios, Peter Lancelot. 2003. Declaring Victory: Towards Conrad's Poetics of Democracy. *Conradiana* 35 (3): 145–183.

Vanderwielen, Betty. 1994. Gender Performance in *Victory*. *Conradiana: A Journal of Joseph Conrad Studies* 26 (2–3): 201–210.

CHAPTER 4

The Victorian Woman Suicide: "The Idiots," *The Secret Agent*, and *Chance*

"The hem of her skirt seemed to float over that awful sheer drop, she was so close to the edge," recalls Marlow of Flora de Barral, the heroine of *Chance*, who, ill-served by the nineteenth-century ideal of benevolent paternalism, contemplates suicide (Conrad 1924a, 43). The striking image of a skirt on the edge of the quarry, a representation of her fragile femininity with its floating hem, effectively dramatizes the brutal death that even a step would confer. Having lost her scheming lover, her manipulative governess, and the prestige and wealth offered by her father's former position, Flora is on the edge, metaphorically as well as literally, struggling with her identity and future social role. As a pure young woman mired in her father's dishonor and her guardian's cruelty, Flora appears to be a variation on the figure of the disgraced suicidal woman, familiar from Victorian art and literature, since these betrayals make her hopeless and uncertain of her place.

"The Idiots," *The Secret Agent*, and *Chance* each develop a critique of Victorian gender roles though representations of the woman suicide, sympathetically portraying the heroine's struggles against her proscribed role and its absurd limitations. The heroines of "The Idiots" and *The Secret Agent* drown themselves at the conclusion of their respective texts in a final hopeless gesture against society that also marks the limits of conventional narrative. In *Chance*, the heroine considers suicide repeatedly, yet she chooses to live and ultimately to remarry, fulfilling some version of the happy marriage plot, even as the novel invites criticism of such a resolution. The figure of the nineteenth-century female suicide,

© The Author(s) 2017
E.B. Harrington, *Conrad's Sensational Heroines*,
DOI 10.1007/978-3-319-63297-1_4

a young woman who drowns herself to escape disgrace, becomes familiar from the 1840s onward, depicted as a poignant moral reminder for
women to value their purity (Nicoletti 2004, 9).[1] This image figures
prominently in "The Idiots" and in *The Secret Agent*, although Conrad's
approach, tempered with irony, departs from the familiar, sentimentalized notion of the tragic woman. The suicides in these narratives are not
unwed mothers but married women who have killed their husbands, and,
despite the seriousness of the crimes, Conrad frames their drownings as
the remedy to the impossible liberation provided by the crime, working against the expected depiction of the drowned woman. Reflecting
on the disgrace implicit in the original image, Conrad uses the figure of
the female suicide to pose a social critique, inviting sympathy for these
murderous heroines by acknowledging that their circumstances are not
entirely of their own making.

In some ways, *Chance* might be said to begin where the earlier narratives leave off, posing an alternative to suicide for Flora, who considers
suicide at several significant junctures in the text. Her circumstances illuminate the way in which her infantilizing upbringing leaves her unprepared for the kind of worldly self-interest that her father, her governess,
and her suitor represent. After Marlow's call, she draws back from the
edge, yet that resonant image immediately comes to mind when he
returns to visit the Fynes on the night she has disappeared. Invited to
envision Flora's suicide as the completion of the earlier scene, the reader
soon realizes with Marlow that Flora has actually run away to start a new
life, rather than end her life.

The repeated possibility of her suicide forms the beginning of the
heroine's story in *Chance*. Feeling worthless, betrayed, and unlovable,
Flora accepts that suicide is an appropriate remedy for a Victorian woman's dishonor, self-destruction becoming a means for a generally passive
woman to protest, or at least abandon, her subordinate position in the
patriarchal system. Furthermore, in developing Marlow's perspective on

---

[1] As L.J. Nicoletti (2007) explains: "Victorian Londoners were inundated with images of
drowned women" that resembled each other in popular representations: "Early in the era,
the iconography became well established and ahistoric: a composition framed by an arch;
a moonlit setting; a beautiful, unscathed corpse; and a fall from Blackfriars or Waterloo
bridge, allowing St. Paul's Cathedral to be moralistically included in the background."
Until the 1840s, the iconography of suicide was more associated with men, who remained
more likely to commit suicide than women throughout the period (Nicoletti 2004, 8).

Flora in *Chance*, Conrad draws attention to the process of storytelling, drawing from popular narratives and representations of women in a tale told by a contradictory, often unfamiliar, version of Marlow, who veers from being sympathetic to being strident.

As Owen Knowles and Gene M. Moore (2000) note, "*Chance* has arguably the happiest ending of all of Conrad's novels," which comes in striking contrast to many other Conrad narratives (58). Through the character of Flora, Conrad revisits the heroines of "The Idiots" and *The Secret Agent* (which are themselves, arguably, versions of the same story), creating a character that survives her disgrace and flourishes. Conrad apparently began writing *Chance* before *The Secret Agent* and then picked it up again, completing it in 1911, so the novels naturally treat similar themes.[2] When Conrad committed to publish *Chance* in the *New York Herald*, he transformed the text to appeal to a wider audience including a female readership (Jones 1999, 144–145). Certainly, the narratives of "The Idiots," *The Secret Agent*, and *Chance* have some strong similarities, particularly with regard to the treatment of women's roles and choices, and considering Conrad's examination of gender politics, feminism, and patriarchy through the portrayal of suicide in these texts offers us a complex perspective on his position on these issues.

Both "The Idiots" and *The Secret Agent* feature doom-laden endings for their heroines, the former melodramatic, the latter more nihilistic, that mark the hopelessness of the heroine's violent revolt against the patriarchal figures who have failed her. Indeed, the treatment of the suicides of Susan Bacadou and Winnie Verloc has a grimly comic tone, the culmination of an absurd series of events in which each woman kills her husband to assert her autonomy in a kind of exaggerated refusal to consent to marital sex. Though each killing occurs under duress—Susan, threatened with rape by her husband, does not want to conceive another mentally disabled child to add to her brood, and Winnie has just discovered that her cowardly husband caused her mentally disabled brother's

---

[2] "The Idiots" was published in 1896. *The Secret Agent* was written after Conrad apparently began writing *Chance* in 1905; once he completed *The Secret Agent* in 1906, he went back to *Chance* several times starting in 1907, finally completing it in 1911 (Hampson 1992, 196). Susan Jones (1999) traces *Chance* to the early, unfinished short story "Dynamite," to which Conrad refers in correspondence in 1898 and 1899 (135). According to Jones, the manuscript of *Chance* in the Berg collection of the New York Public Library has an attached note that states this version was begun in 1906 (136, n7).

death—the women immediately recognize that the future can hold nothing for them, since their crimes alienate them not only from society, but also from their ingrained understanding of their identity as women and wives.

The possibility of Flora's suicide may be read as an ironic reframing of these earlier endings that acts as a point of departure for the rich possibilities of Flora's future life. *Chance* departs from the dark renderings of marital strife in the other two fictions to bring a more hopeful vision of marriage and even the possibility of a second chance at happiness, a resolution unimaginable in the dark worlds of "The Idiots" and *The Secret Agent*. Yet this ending is undermined by the famous complexity of the narration, "the protagonist caught within a web of male perspectives on women," that critiques the genre of romance fiction even as it borrows its plots (Jones 1999, 102). At the end of the story, we know that Marlow has supplied a resolution, quite literally by facilitating it, but we do not know that his version of the story is authoritative; Conrad seems to offer us the kind of conventional Victorian ending against which his more modernist treatment of Marlow's narrative works. The title, *Chance*, suggests that the happy ending, as well as the circumstances that avert Flora's contemplation of suicide, occurs only by good fortune, since women's situation in general has not changed; thus, it can be read as a comment on the contrived situations and reversals of conventional romance. By leaving Flora's survival and the novel's resolution to chance, Conrad invites readers to critique the formulaic genre and its typical perspective on women. *Chance*'s proffered happy ending enables an appraisal of genre that might undermine the reliability of the portrayal of Flora, offering the kind of self-conscious assessment of genre that recalls *The Secret Agent* even as it relieves the heroine's need to kill herself by developing a different plot.

I

The heroine's suicide at the end of "The Idiots" serves as a relief from the implacable conflict of the story; as an obedient wife, Susan Bacadou cannot refuse her husband's demands for sex, yet her fear of additional procreation is so great that she kills him by way of objection (Conrad 1924b). As discussed in the second chapter, the stresses of raising four mentally disadvantaged children in "The Idiots" leads to the deterioration of the Bacadou family and the death of both parents. Susan's domestic role is defined largely by her mothering of their children, while Jean-Pierre's outside work as a farmer is more influenced by the lack of the assistance his sons should bring. Her husband's insistence that they should conceive another child puts her in direct conflict with the patriarchal authority that he both reveres and represents, so much so that she sees killing her husband as less of a sin than bearing another child. Susan is shocked by both the failures of the church and of God to allay her suffering. In comparing "The Idiots" to a likely source, Maupassant's "La Mère aux monstres,"[3] Gene Moore (1997) notes: "[A] point of similarity can be found in the manner in which both stories seek to exculpate the mothers by delivering a moral indictment of the worlds within which they live. If the mothers deserve blame as 'horrible' or 'diabolical' women, both stories strongly imply that they have been rendered 'monstrous' by social and economic constraints beyond their control" (54). Perhaps because Susan feels her maternal burdens severely and judges her children harshly as "things," she kills her husband as an affirmation of ownership over her body and her choices, if only to end her life in the next hours (Conrad 1924b, 76). Her mother comments cruelly and perceptively after the murder, "There is no room for you in this world" (77). Despite the characteristic irony in the mild, faithful Susan's murder-suicide, "The Idiots" emphasizes her desperation and struggle with the requisite submission of the wifely role. After her own mother's rejection and despite her sense of the rightness of killing her husband, Susan runs into the tide to die in the water, convinced she is pursued by her dead husband. She calls to the man trying to save her, thinking he is the spectre of her husband: "I want to live. To live alone—for a week—for a day. I must explain to them" (84), a plea to escape her suffocating role if only for a few hours. Yet, this desire for freedom and for space is impossible in the circumstances; she can only go into the water.

The domestic plot of *The Secret Agent* also features a wife who murders her husband because of his poor stewardship of a mentally disabled child; Winnie Verloc then commits suicide after finding that her newfound freedom holds nothing for her (Conrad 1924c). However, *The Secret Agent* offers a fuller, darker social critique of individual hypocrisy and self-interest, connecting a singularly corrupt and cynical political and

---

[3] The story is based in part on Conrad's experience of a similar community with disabled children in Brittany on his honeymoon (see Stape and Simmons 2011).

civic realm with the personal tragedy of Stevie's death and the murder-suicide that follows. Certainly, both Winnie Verloc and Susan Bacadou are apparently submissive wives not given to self-examination who reach a breaking point and react with violence. After Winnie, somnambulant in her shock, murders her husband, she immediately offers herself to another protector, unable to imagine fleeing on her own or even acting on her own behalf. Ultimately, she throws herself off the "cross-Channel Boat" (Conrad 1924c, 307). The act of suicide is absent from the text, and Winnie's drowning is represented by the engraved wedding ring she removes prior to killing herself. Whether obtrusively shining in their "dust-bin" of a pornography shop or surrendered in the moments before her suicide as the only way to fully disentangle herself from the marriage that was intended to be a convenience, the ring remains the glittering emblem of a marriage made impossible by the blind self-interest of both parties (213). Such conflicts of private self-interest often characterize the marital relationships in Conrad's world.

In *The Secret Agent*, the elopement plot that rescues Flora in *Chance* is ironically inverted: when Winnie Verloc, running from her crime, is robbed and spurned by the increasingly, comically fearful Ossipon, she drowns herself. She had cried out to him earlier "I will live out all my days for you, Tom!" in what becomes a horrific parody, a hastily given lover's pledge after her murder of her husband (298). Winnie and Flora have been betrayed by their fathers and guardians and are pushed into familiar sensationalized roles: Winnie turns murderess over her horrible loss and betrayal, and Flora, victimized, contemplates suicide after her father's downfall and her subsequent betrayal by her governess and her suitor. Like Susan Bacadou, these heroines exemplify Conrad's critique of the patriarchal system that leaves women in the care of men who fail to understand them or even consider them empathetically.

Thus, Conrad explores the combination of sympathy and stigma bound up in representations of the female suicide, foregrounding the idea of problematic sexuality bound up in premarital sex and disgrace. Susan refuses sex by retaliating against her husband's threatened violence with violence; Winnie barters herself in her marriage of convenience, then refuses sex after Stevie's death, longing for freedom like Susan, but her first act as a "free" woman is to try to offer herself to Ossipon more cheaply. Sexuality and social dishonor are again connected to the decision to commit suicide, yet Conrad's frank treatment of the circumstances surrounding the suicides works against the customary reductive reading of disgrace familiar from the image of the woman suicide. The outrageous provocation of Susan's and Winnie's violence invites sympathy by critiquing their limited options and lack of freedom prior to the murders. For Flora, the recurring contemplation of suicide reaffirms the "miserable dependence of girls," since Flora has been raised to be sheltered in a traditional feminine role that leaves her unable to stand up for herself or even to comprehend fully her family disgrace as it unfolds (*C* 172).

II

Comparing *Chance* and *The Secret Agent*, Leland Monk (1993) notes that there is "every indication" that Flora is dead as Marlow and Fyne go to look for her, but *Chance* develops alternative possibilities, in contrast to the determinism of Verloc's and Winnie's fates in *The Secret Agent*. Monk explains, "But in Flora's case the expectations conjured up by the descriptive, figural, and punning language [present in both novels] are not realized" (97–98). Throughout *Chance*, Conrad alludes to the plot developments and gender issues that are at the heart of *The Secret Agent*, yet refigures them into a narrative that, far from the "ironic method" and black comedy of the earlier novel ("Author's Note" to *SA*, xiii) poses the possibility of personal growth and development. Indeed, Jones (1999) argues that *Chance* can be read as a *Bildungsroman* (117). By the end of the novel, *The Secret Agent* has presented a hopeless series of female roles that seem to exhaust the heroine's range of possible identities, culled from the sensational novel, as she drowns herself.

   Chance borrows these primary plot points from *The Secret Agent* but alters their significance: a woman's selflessness for a male relative, the abandonment of a dangerously greedy suitor, the potential for atavism, the empty promise of women's liberation, and a marriage of convenience are woven into a narrative that counters the nihilism of *The Secret Agent* with a probing, speculative consideration of gender identity. Flora de Barral is repeatedly rescued, surviving the threat of being abandoned or becoming a suicide, and, even in her eventual widowhood, the novel depicts the promise, rather than the tragedy, of her future life. Thus, Conrad complicates the dark Darwinism of *The Secret Agent* with a vision of the adaptive possibility of the heroine in a world still defined by traditional gender roles and the chivalric fantasies that surround them. Continuing his critique of *fin-de-siècle* feminism from *The Secret Agent* in *Chance*, Conrad recasts his hopeless vision of the "free woman" from the former novel by revisiting the notion of women's liberation. Marlow translates Mrs. Fyne's feminism as the theory that women should "turn themselves into unscrupulous, sexless nuisances," mocking the pretense that women can extricate themselves from their existing social roles merely by opposing them (*C* 190).

In *Chance*, Flora repeatedly considers suicide, since her father's disgrace leaves her bereft—ashamed and in poverty, with a strong sense of her own worthlessness. After his downfall and incarceration, she is cast out by his cousins, abandoned at the Fynes' house and has to be restrained from fleeing into the street "with the haste, I suppose, of despair and to keep I don't know what tragic tryst" (177). When she does not succeed as a lady's companion, the Fynes help her to find another position with a German family. After being unfairly cast out by the family for whom she is serving as governess, Flora considers suicide: "If it had not been for the stewardess who, without asking questions, good soul, took charge of her quietly in the ladies' saloon (luckily it was empty) it is by no means certain she would ever have reached England. … Suicide, I suspect, is very often the outcome of mere mental weariness—not an act of savage energy but the final symptom of complete collapse" (182–183). This scene echoes Winnie's demise in many details: in *The Secret Agent*, the kind and watchful stewardess leaves to arrange for Winnie's care, ironically allowing her the time to kill herself unobserved, but in *Chance*, the stewardess intervenes to stop Flora's self-destruction. Marlow takes care to characterize the contemplated act as derived from exhaustion and "collapse" rather than from violence, a description that, like the "tragic tryst" he mentions earlier, recalls the familiar image of the female suicide, two versions of the seductiveness of death for a disgraced woman (183, 177). Then Marlow himself witnesses Flora's near attempt at the quarry and intervenes, though she claims not to have been deterred by Marlow so much as the fear that the Fynes' dog, her companion on her walk, would follow her leap into the quarry and die as well. Flora plans another suicide attempt at the quarry but Roderick Anthony, unaware of her intention, joins her in her walk and prevents her attempt. She again plans suicide even after Anthony professes his love, but she encounters him in the garden, waiting for her reply, and chooses to elope with him rather than kill herself. When she is discovered to be missing, Marlow fears she has returned to the quarry to throw herself down, and Fyne and Marlow search for her. When the Fynes realize she has eloped with Mrs. Fyne's brother, Roderick Anthony, Flora is again pursued, but this time with Mrs. Fyne's venom for having taken up with her brother. Finally, after her marriage and her father's release from prison, she decides that, if her unwilling father "bolts" rather than embarks on the ship, she will "jump into the dock. That at least won't lie" (370). Confiding in Marlow, she offers relatively little commentary on the recurring suicidal thoughts, but here explains that her suicide would be a means of expressing herself, of telling the truth. In her desperation, she considers suicide a preferable way to resolve the miscommunication and misunderstandings in relationships with her father and Anthony, as she is caught between the two men's misreadings and idealizations of her. Yet her story here is, of course, told still through Marlow's perceptions of her: As Jeremy Hawthorn (1990) wryly notes, "The reader is left hungering for a fuller view of Flora de Barral and Roderick Anthony, and hoping for less of Marlow" (146).

Flora does not commit suicide or even attempt it, yet *Chance* repeatedly alludes to her contemplation of suicide, returning to consider and reconsider her desire to kill herself as her story is fleshed out in the narration. In his study of suicide in Conrad and Ford Madox Ford, Anthony Fothergill (2003) explores the notion of repetition in relation to suicide, arguing that "rehearsal and repetition are bound up with actual and literary suicide": "Through remembering and re-telling, we seek to explain or do justice to an ending that is not a 'proper' end. And where repetition plays a vital role in the quest to understand, literature is uniquely placed to help, offering narrative re-plays which make available imaginative contexts for the act by retracing the events (or non-events) and the motivations (or their absence) which culminate in suicide" (179). Although Fothergill does not consider *Chance* in his study, the novel's "rehearsal and repetition" of the possibility of Flora's suicide serve to develop her character in the context of her desire to end her life while substituting a "'proper' end," so that suicide does not necessarily become a defining quality in her character as it does for Susan and Winnie. Fothergill explains that while "outside observers (be they coroners, theologians, psychologists, news reporters or friends)" consider a life backwards from a suicide reductively, "The novelist, in contrast, can rehearse the fabric, the fuller texture and complexity of the life, creating for the reader the impression of the life folding into an unknown future which *might* end in such a death" (195). The chances that hinder Flora's suicide attempts enable her to develop an alternate resolution, this uniquely happy ending. The repetition emphasizes not only the depth of her despair, developing a perspective on her psychological makeup, but also the social causes for her frustrating position, as Conrad develops them in his indictment of patriarchy. (Indeed, it seems almost as if Flora's father's suicide relieves her of the need to commit suicide herself.) The novel repeatedly shows Flora's frustration with the limits of her imposed role; she is no better served by Mrs. Fyne's feminism than by her father's patriarchal possessiveness.

Titling the two parts of the novel "The Damsel" and "The Knight," Conrad makes explicit his formulaic frame of reference, but, as Jones (1999) explains:

> Far from capitulating to the formulaic romance, the final version of *Chance* offers a challenging portrait of psychological isolation in a woman, subverting generic expectations and questioning assumptions about gender. [...] In *Chance*, the repetition of well-worn gestures and poses reinforces the reader's perception of a gap between being and representation, drawing attention to the disparity between what a woman is, or might choose to be, and the roles that have been prescribed for her. (102)

Indeed, the novel draws Flora's governess and Mrs. Fyne, not only as failed companions and maternal figures for Flora, but also as stereotyped examples of contemporary femininity. The governess, who "was nearly forty and harboured a secret taste for patronizing young men of sorts— of a certain sort" (73), might resemble the mercenary villainesses of nineteenth-century sensation fiction, but she can also be read as a caricature of the liberated femininity of the *fin de siècle*. In cultivating relationships with young men, she prioritizes her own desires, yet her cruelly mercenary actions indicate that she is estranged from any maternal sensibility toward or sisterly comradeship with Flora. Marlow notes, "When a woman takes to any unlawful sort of man-trade, there's nothing to beat her in the way of thoroughness" (93). In this generalization, framed as a proverb, Marlow criticizes the "plotting governess with the trick of a 'perfect lady' manner" for taking to a kind of "man-trade," or operating with the scheming, greedy sensibility of men in the marketplace in a way that is unnatural for women and compromises her femininity (93). Flora recounts that she had "the feeling of being personally attacked" by the governess, and Marlow continues, "It was only because of the girl being so much of a child that she escaped mental destruction" (117).

Indeed, Flora has been so isolated and infantilized that she is unable to recognize the governess's innate cruelty and her scheme to marry Flora to her pretended nephew for her own enrichment. Her idealized purity renders her sympathetic to the reader but also absurd. Flora represents Victorian female dependency without proper guardianship, and her situation implicitly critiques the social ideals she embodies. As Jones argues, Conrad here exposes the gap between Flora and her "prescribed" roles, a gap that will widen as she is abandoned and must confront her newly lowered position.

After Flora's vulgar middle-class relative, her father's cousin, comes to collect her, Mrs. Fyne recollects the scene: "'She never looked back at us,' said Mrs. Fyne. 'She just followed him out. I've never had such a crushing impression of the miserable dependence of girls—of women. This was an extreme case. But a young man—any man—could have gone to break stones on the roads or something of that kind—or enlisted—or—'" (172). Thus, Conrad makes clear the problems with women's inability to make their own way in the world; constrained by her role as a Victorian woman, she cannot "break stones" but must simply submit to the disgrace that comes with her father's crimes. Like Winnie, Flora initially cannot envision another "road." Even as Marlow seems to lament Flora's limited options along with Mrs. Fyne, he remains highly critical of the caricature of closed-minded feminism she signifies. He lectures her husband Fyne about the "vengeful" "sort of moral sword-and-fire doctrine" she represents to Marlow and complains that Mrs. Fyne "can't forgive Miss de Barral for being a woman and behaving like a woman" (187–188). Mrs. Fyne is a character of "farce," comic and "incapable of tragedy" (Luyat 1980, 10). Here, as in Marlow's description of the governess, Zoe Fyne has a mannish quality that he sees as threatening to Flora, and he characterizes Mrs. Fyne's feminist doctrine as something that makes women "unscrupulous" and "sexless" (190). Even as Marlow acknowledges the unfairness of Flora's position as a woman, he reacts powerfully against the idea of women's liberation, instead reinscribing the chivalrous ideal. Paul Armstrong (1993) explains, "What most offends and disturbs Marlow about Mrs. Fyne's feminism is the way it bonds her with others of her sex. ... Mrs. Fyne's relations with her 'girl-friends' establish an exclusive community of women in accord with the lesbian ethos of some kinds of radical feminism" (167). Even outside of Marlow's extreme reaction to Mrs. Fyne, this bonding, evoking a kind of sexualized sisterhood, is problematized in the novel.

The cynical, caricatured portrayal of Mrs. Fyne in *Chance* seems to follow Conrad's critique of *fin-de-siècle* feminism and the New Woman from *The Secret Agent*. The repeated description of Winnie after Stevie's death and the murder of Verloc as a "free woman," despite her traumatized, trance-like state in those scenes, mockingly portrays her newfound liberation. Though Winnie has been betrayed by the husband who was supposed to be a protector for her and Stevie, much as she and Stevie were betrayed by their abusive father, Conrad treats women's liberation sceptically in the novel as a state as untenable as the wifely role Winnie has abandoned. Freedom from Verloc and from responsibility for Stevie does not confer, in itself, liberation, and Winnie is shown to be as ideologically imprisoned as those "German slaves" and "downtrodden slaves" that she mentions elsewhere in the novel (60, 205). Both *The Secret Agent* and *Chance* frankly portray the problems with women's submissive role alongside their critique of feminism.

III

When Allan Simmons (1999) notes that "Structurally, Marlow's misogyny offers a counterpoint to Mrs. Fyne's feminism," he invites us to consider that Conrad presents both Marlow's misogyny and Mrs. Fyne's stereotyped feminism as suspect positions (262). While Marlow's perspective as narrator dominates, it is inconsistent, offering offensive generalizations about men as well as women, and discussing Marlow's own femininity at times. As Marlow explains, women are again the keepers of "certain well-known, well-established, I'll almost say hackneyed, illusions, without which the average male creature cannot get on" (94). Without disavowing his perspective, Conrad offers us room to critique Marlow: "Marlow does not escape unchallenged. He belongs to the company of imperfect mentors that fills the book—the fathers, the governess, Mrs. Fyne" (Davies 1993, 88). Despite their negative attributes, it is through this series of "imperfect mentors" that some kind of education for Flora, and perhaps progress, can occur in *Chance*.

This notion of progress builds on the nineteenth-century novel trope of the orphan who gains a future in part by coming to terms with the past. In his fragmented, alliterative description of De Barral and his daughter Flora at her mother's grave, Conrad underscores his allusions to Dickens in *Chance*: "Figures from Dickens—pregnant with pathos" (162). *The Secret Agent* also draws attention to the various roles and poses women occupy, often drawn from the pages of nineteenth-century fiction, including that of Dickens, and the novel emphasizes the ways in which such expectations shape women's thinking about themselves and their actions that follow. As noted in the first chapter, Winnie has followed the general wisdom offered to Victorian wives: she is submissive, maternal, devoted to her home and her husband's domestic comforts, and notably uncurious about his work-life and late-night destinations. Yet this performance of the domestic role has not guaranteed her the security that she believed would follow from her marital bargain. As detached as Winnie seems for much of the novel, refusing to involve herself too deeply in anything until circumstances demand it, her character invites sympathy as she faces the reality of Stevie's death. As in the sensation fiction of the 1860s upon which Conrad draws, Winnie's brutal crime, the murder of her husband, is recast for the reader in the awareness of her limited options and the failings of the men in her life.

Chance, The Secret Agent, and "The Idiots" use these specific critiques of fatherly failing to illustrate the larger failings of society with regard to women. The flawed figures of De Barral and Carleon Anthony loom over Chance. Conrad's portrayal of Carleon Anthony, famously a parody of the nineteenth-century poet Coventry Patmore, offers a clear critique of the oppressive nature of Victorian femininity as the idealizing poet acts as a "domestic tyrant" at home (C 62). De Barral, heedless of the sacrifices his idealizing daughter has made for him, would happily murder her husband and sacrifice her happiness for liberty from his upright son-in-law; he is unabashed by his conviction and prison term and remains selfish and self-righteous until his suicide when his last gambit fails. Flora's growth and sexual maturity are impaired by her father's possessiveness over her sexuality, as he judges her husband a rival for his daughter.

In the logic of the text, De Barral must be removed for Flora and Roderick Anthony to achieve a normal sexual relationship and a satisfying marriage. The focus on a problematic paternal legacy also carries into the heedless, petty tyrants in The Secret Agent. Winnie's father, ashamed and abusive of his mentally disabled son Stevie, beats him, thus forcing his daughter to stand up to his abuse in protecting her brother. The "bed of compassion" that Winnie provides, a place free of fear of abuse, also represents the unnatural closeness that his brutal fatherliness fosters between the children (168). (In Chance, this quasi-incestuous closeness is reflected in Mrs. Fyne's possessiveness of her brother, Roderick Anthony, which manifests itself in her anger and jealousy at his elopement with Flora). Likewise, the self-absorbed Verloc can never see Stevie as an adopted son—in the highly ironic narration, Verloc extends only "as much recognition to Stevie as a man not particularly fond of animals may give to his wife's beloved cat" (39)—nor understand Winnie's adoring, motherly attachment to him. Verloc uses Stevie as a pawn to remove the embassy pressure on him, never considering the personal risk to the boy, nor his own responsibility to Stevie. "The Idiots" presents Jean-Pierre Bacadou as disengaged from his children and unconcerned with the ethics of continuing to father disabled children; his only concern is that he have both practical assistance with the farm and the psychological reassurance of passing on his birthright, the land he works, to a son.

Neither "The Idiots" nor *The Secret Agent* ends with the image of the drowned woman, although this figure precipitates the resolution of each story. "The Idiots" finishes with Susan's mother, Madame Levaille, reflecting on her daughter's death as the Marquis de Chavanes reassures her he will use his influence to have the curé consider Susan's death accidental, so she can be buried in consecrated ground. Susan had longed for her faith to rescue her and give her a normal child to no avail, and had grown increasingly frustrated with the patriarchal submission the church requires, but here Conrad shows the church to be a practical, malleable institution quite different from Susan's understanding of it. The Marquis uses his influence to have Susan buried in the churchyard because he wants her businesswoman mother to be appointed administrator of the estate to keep it out of the hands of the Bacadous, who might be Republicans. Thus, the conclusion emphasizes the critique of patriarchy that runs through the story: Jean-Pierre's hopes for his land are thoroughly dashed as it reverts to his mother-in-law in service of the old order, which is allied with the church he despises. Neither the Republican Jean-Pierre nor the institutions of Church and State had anything to offer Susan, who longed to live and to live alone for a time. Even Susan's mother is a caricature of the bourgeois individualist, a businesswoman who cares only about reputation and financial success and has little sentiment to spare for her struggling daughter.

The Secret Agent, too, touches on Winnie's estate, the disposition of her money and the effect of her death on the man who abandoned her. Ossipon is famous for his parasitic treatment of women, but the Professor's mocking of Ossipon's sentiment at Winnie's death exposes the weakness the Professor sees in him, a character whose ego and self-involvement had hitherto seemed absolute. The Professor shows Ossipon the logical extension of his grasping, manipulative ways to no avail, as he gradually loses his ability to function. Ossipon becomes so repulsed by Winnie's money that he agrees to use it to finance the Professor's anarchist bombs, proffered to anyone who requests one and ironically replenishing the source of the bomb that killed Winnie's brother. While Ossipon's regret for Winnie might be characterized as growth, the first evidence of altruistic sentiment, it leads only to his self-destruction or "ruin" as he describes it (310). In contrast, the characterization of Winnie offers no evidence of growth, since her killing of Verloc is atavistic, almost instinctive, and the freedom that she longs for after Stevie's death can culminate in nothing more than an immediate attempt to find another man to help her. Thus, Conrad's powerful presentation of her impossible role, her inability to create her own life—or even flee on her own—and the critique of patriarchy he develops are tempered by his rendering of women's liberation as absurd in a society whose gender roles are so imprisoning and pervasive.

While *Chance* acknowledges the difficulties of women's submissive role, the novel ends on a note of optimism, giving Flora the chance to live on her own as Susan longed to live, but then implying that her being alone can be remedied by a new marriage to Powell. Once her father dies, Flora learns how to live with Roderick Anthony and then as a widow without resorting to suicide. As Marlow is able to encourage the relationship between the widowed Flora and the admiring Powell in *Chance*, Conrad tempers the melodramatic tragedy of Anthony's accidental drowning with the possibility of Flora's future happiness with another man. By facilitating real communication and personal growth, Marlow, depicted in the text as misogynistic and imprisoned by his own illusions and ideologies about gender, seems to assist the characters to transcend the determinism that might inflect the ending of the novel. Yet the very complexity of the narration seems to undermine the credibility of this resolution. Marlow has been in dialogue with the narrator about his viewpoints and, by extension, his limitations as a storyteller throughout *Chance*. If anything, his own account makes the ending more suspect, since it seems to rely upon a romantic ending in which a new knight (or two, counting Marlow) does service to the damsel, ensuring that she not remain problematically single for long.

The emphasis on Flora's suicide attempts might be read as Marlow's replaying of a familiar narrative of female disgrace and suicide as a way to dramatize his vision of Flora's violated purity, although she is able to escape this end. Jones (1999) argues that, ultimately, this attempt "to shape the heroine's story according to the conventions of a traditional romance" fails, and that Flora is finally liberated from their expectations (126). So, it follows that Flora may become another kind of "free woman" liberated from the conventions of genre, if not entirely society's conventions. Conrad's social critique resounds in his return to the familiar sensational elements, the bitterness over Mrs. Fyne's philosophy partially eclipsed by the sympathetic presentation of Flora's initially harsh life experience. Flora does get to live as a free woman, and one who relishes her later life. By leaving us with the promise of her remarriage, rather than the bitter triumph of an Ossipon-like suitor, Conrad invites us to read *Chance* as a departure, although admittedly one that, according to convention, mistrusts her ability to be happy on her own. His reprising of these narrative elements from "The Idiots" and *The Secret Agent* marks a departure from its fatalism, and the complexity of this re-envisioning of the heroine offers much more than the touted romance meant to garner readers for the *New York Herald*.

REFERENCES

Armstrong, Paul. 1993. "Misogyny and the Ethics of Reading: The Problem of Conrad's *Chance*." In *Contexts for Conrad*, ed. Keith Carabine, Owen Knowles, and Wiesław Krajka, 151–174. Boulder: Eastern European Monographs.

Conrad, Joseph. 1924a. *Chance: A Tale in Two Parts*. Garden City: Doubleday, Page, and Company.

———. 1924b. "The Idiots." In *Tales of Unrest*, 93–142. Garden City: Doubleday, Page, and Company.

———. 1924c. *The Secret Agent: A Simple Tale*. Garden City: Doubleday, Page, and Company.

Davies, Laurence. 1993. "Conrad, Chance, and Women Readers." In *Conrad and Gender*, ed. Andrew Michael Roberts, 75–88. Amsterdam: Rodopi.

Fothergill, Anthony. 2003. "'For to End Yet Again': Suicide in the Stories of Joseph Conrad and Ford Madox Ford." In *Inter-Relations: Conrad, James, Ford and Others*, ed. Keith Carabine and Max Saunders, 179–208. Boulder: Social Science Monographs.

Hampson, Robert. 1992. *Joseph Conrad: Betrayal and Identity*. New York: St. Martin's Press.

Hawthorn, Jeremy. 1990. *Joseph Conrad: Narrative Technique and Ideological Commitment.* London: Edward Arnold.

Jones, Susan. 1999. *Conrad and Women.* Oxford: Oxford University Press.

Knowles, Owen, and Gene M. Moore. 2000. *"Chance."* In *Oxford Reader's Companion to Conrad,* ed. Owen Knowles and Gene M. Moore, 58–61. Oxford: Oxford University Press.

Luyat, Anne. 1980. Conrad's Feminine Grotesques. *The Conradian* 6 (2): 5–15.

Monk, Leland. 1993. *Standard Deviations: Chance and the Modern British Novel.* Stanford: Stanford University Press.

Moore, Gene M. 1997. "Conrad's 'The Idiots' and Maupassant's 'La Mère au monstres.'" In *Conrad Intertexts and Appropriations: Essays in Memory of Yves Hervouet,* ed. Gene M. Moore., Owen Knowles., and J.H. Stape, 49–58. Amsterdam, Netherlands: Rodopi.

Nicoletti, L.J. 2004. "Downward Mobility: Victorian Women, Suicide, and London's "Bridge of Sighs." *Literary London: Interdisciplinary Studies in the Representation of London* 2 (1): n. p. Accessed Apr 17, 2017. http://www. literarylondon.org/london-journal/march2004/nicoletti.html.

Nicoletti. 2007. "Morbid Topographies: Placing Suicide in Victorian London." In *A Mighty Mass of Brick and Stone: Victorian and Edwardian Representations of London,* ed. Lawrence Phillips, 7–34. Amsterdam: Rodopi.

Simmons, Allan. 1999. "The Later Novels: *Chance* (1913), *The Arrow of Gold* (1919), *The Rescue* (1920), *The Rover* (1923), and *Suspense* (1925)." In *A Joseph Conrad Companion,* ed. Leonard Orr and Ted Billy, 252–280. Westport, Connecticut: Greenwood Press.

Stape, J.H. and Allan H. Simmons. 2011. "The Conrads in Brittany: Some Biographical Notes." *The Conradian* 36 (1): 70–79.

CHAPTER 5

The Fallen Woman and Sexuality as "Their Own Weapon": *Victory*, "Because of the Dollars," and *The Arrow of Gold*

Late in the novel *Victory*, its protagonist, Axel Heyst, himself the victim of false and venomous mischaracterizations by another character, turns on his lover Lena with a surprising and bitter screed: "No doubt you acted from instinct. Women have been provided with their own weapon. I was a disarmed man. I have been a disarmed man all my life—as I see it now. For you the glory of resourcefulness and of a profound knowledge of yourself. But I must say that the other attitude, suggestive of shame, had its charm. For you are full of charm!" (Conrad 2016, 345). Heyst, whose attitude toward Lena has hitherto been marked by compassion and generosity, as well as a depth of emotion that is discomfiting for him, seems almost to be reading from a script that condescends to women as purveyors of a base "instinctual" sexuality that "disarms" and victimizes men, here cast as a kind of evolutionary weakness in the male. This scripted quality is partly due to Conrad's self-conscious evocation of popular genre fiction throughout the novel, particularly in the melodramatic plotting and the sometimes deliberately overblown language of the final chapters from which this quotation is taken. But it is also due to Heyst's presumption that a baser, "fallen" woman must underlie the more modern, resourceful and self-aware Lena, the heroine who is literally dying to save him in this scene. Despite Heyst's noted dissimilarity from the men who try repeatedly to victimize Lena, he invokes the same stereotypes about women that underlie their behavior. In Heyst's accusation, women are able to manipulate men "by instinct" using their sexuality atavistically to threaten the more civilized, rational male, a model that recalls that Victorian reading

© The Author(s) 2017   77
E.B. Harrington, *Conrad's Sensational Heroines*,
DOI 10.1007/978-3-319-63297-1_5

of such "fallen" women who have sex outside of marriage (and, thus, fall from God's grace) as sexual aggressors who potentially threaten men's autonomy.[1] By marking the absurdity of Heyst's position as well as Lena's untenable situation, Conrad's potent use of irony in *Victory* reveals a notable critique of patriarchy and the ideological forces promulgated in the popular novel. Furthermore, by implicitly questioning the traditional linking of women's extramarital sexuality with dishonor, Conrad considers the ramifications of the New Woman figure and women's increasing autonomy in light of men's struggles to assimilate to the radical cultural changes associated with the early twentieth century. Instead of merely recalling traditional gender roles in these novels, Conrad questions the basis for such roles, highlighting their arbitrary and restrictive nature.

Both *Victory* and *The Arrow of Gold* feature a uniquely desirable woman at the heart of the narrative, one who suffers from the social stigma associated with her sexuality and her desirability. In taking the sexualized and clearly commodified woman as his subject in these novels, Conrad evokes two female categories replete with anxiety, the Victorian fallen woman and the sexually liberated New Woman of the *fin de siècle*. Andrew Michael Roberts (1992) cautiously comments on Conrad's relationship to feminism in *The Arrow of Gold*, noting, "Conrad was deeply implicated with romantic and chivalric ideals, and with a male-centered and hierarchic value-system" but this was tempered by "his highly

---

[1]The category of fallen women might be applied to women in a range of consensual relationships outside of marriage, as well as prostitutes, since women who gratify men's desires—not to mention their own desires—outside of marriage are, in effect, engaging in illicit behavior by contemporary social standards. As William Acton (1857) memorably comments of prostitutes in *Prostitution, Considered in Its Moral, Social, and Sanitary Aspects:*

> Such women, ministers of evil passions, not only gratify desire, but arouse it. Compelled by necessity to seek for customers, they throng our streets and public places, and suggest evil thoughts and desires which might otherwise remain undeveloped. [...T]housands would remain uncontaminated if temptation did not seek them out. Prostitutes have the power of soliciting and tempting. Gunpowder remains harmless until the spark falls upon it; the match, until struck, retains the hidden fire, so lust remains dormant till called into being by an exciting cause. (223)

While Acton's model pointedly describes prostitutes, his gunpowder metaphor demonstrates the role that fallen women in general are presumed to serve in stimulating men's desires and, thus, jeopardizing men's and women's chastity.

developed sense of irony, and of the human tendency to self-deception and manipulation," as well as "his late interest in the representation of women's experience" (532). In representing women's experiences from a critical perspective, however, Conrad takes contemporary anxieties about the empowered woman as a subject in *Victory* and *The Arrow of Gold*, examining the problematic ramifications in the early twentieth century of what Nancy Armstrong (1998) describes as the "double-bodied woman" by considering her intimately through men's eyes (538).

In this chapter, I examine the ways in which *Victory* and *The Arrow of Gold* use the familiar figure of the fallen woman and the frame of the adventure story to consider the ongoing influence of traditional gender roles as a social problem. In each novel, the narration reveals a variety of male viewpoints on women, most of which seem to be informed by what the novels characterize as illusions about women's purity and desirability to which men have been socialized. Both novels show how men's desires objectify these heroines and threaten their autonomy. Lena and Rita are able to temporarily escape the sexual markets that pressure them, taking refuge by going away with sympathetic men. Yet the prevalence of the sexual double standard jeopardizes these newfound relationships as Conrad exposes the residual, entrenched patriarchal thinking that inflects even the well-meaning and compassionate male protagonists; to some extent, each novel demonstrates the ways in which the acceptance of gender categories is requisite to maturation and manhood. While both *Victory* and *The Arrow of Gold* offer a critique of patriarchal attitudes and an ironic, sometimes darkly comic, commentary on the popular narratives that help shape expectations about gender performance, Conrad shows self-realization on the part of these men to be unlikely or imperfect, implying a broader critique of the progress toward manhood requisite to a form like the *Bildungsroman*. Moreover, Conrad depicts women to be subject to similarly destructive illusions and mutual recognition and understanding to be impossible in these narratives. Marianne DeKoven (1991) frames literary modernism in terms of a similar gender divide: "male modernists generally feared the loss of their own hegemony implicit in such a wholesale revision of culture, while female modernists generally feared punishment for their dangerous desire for that revision" (20). In *Victory* and *The Arrow of Gold*, Conrad considers modernist ambivalence about changing gender roles, illuminating the fears DeKoven mentions by representing women's sexuality and struggle for autonomy alongside men's struggle to assimilate to women's new roles in ways for which they are unprepared by their socialization. This invites a self-conscious critique of traditional roles for men and women without, however, envisioning any kind of productive resolution.

I

Conrad's novel *Victory* is plotted as an adventure story, featuring a reluctant, alienated hero; a damsel whose attractiveness and vulnerability cause her peril on multiple occasions; an inscrutable, secretive servant acting for himself; and a band of three brigands of recognizable criminal types, brought together on a the deserted half of a Malaysian island. As with his earlier work, Conrad sketches out a story from this genre only to complicate and subvert its more formulaic expectations, using a non-chronological narrative told from differing narrative viewpoints and allowing the language and style of the novel to critique the generic expectations it evokes. Conrad's intentions here are underscored by the characterization of his central figures: Heyst, an echo of late-nineteenth-century decadence in his "doomed brooding and inertia on Samburan" as he struggles with the troublesome legacy of his father's nihilist philosophy, also cannot help but generously assist individuals suffering in ways he can alleviate, like the penniless Captain Morrison and the lovely, vulnerable Lena (Graham 1996, 208). Commenting on Heyst's escape with Lena, the narrator notes: "Davidson shared my suspicion that this was in its essence the rescue of a distressed human being. Not that we were two romantics, tingeing the world to the hue of our temperament, but that both of us had been acute enough to discover a long time ago that Heyst was" (55). Heyst's struggle with the way his upbringing conflicts with his innate compassion and susceptibility to a kind of romance runs throughout the narrative. Lena's affections are warmed by Heyst's courtesy and compassion with her, since, by her own assessment, she is not "a good girl" (171); at times, Conrad peppers the indirect discourse about Lena with melodramatic images and rapturous language meant to evoke scenes of passion from popular novels which, presumably, have influenced her and culminate in the melodramatic final scene of the novel. Thus, Conrad invites the reader to experience the ensuing adventure plot through the romantic illusions and inevitably problematic expectations of its main characters, the tragic resolution serving as an ironic commentary on the nature of gender expectations and romantic conventions more broadly.

Victory is concerned with European commerce in a small part of Malaysia and the interrelations between its male European inhabitants; unsurprisingly, much of the later plotting centers on Lena, whose sexuality and desirability to men in the islands spur much of the narrative, mirroring and alluding to the other commercial activity that sustains Europeans living there. As the youngest and most attractive member of an all-female European orchestra traveling in the Malay Archipelago (the narration sketches a comic rendering of Schomberg and his pretense of a civic-minded commitment to bringing "artist parties" to his hotel, 52), Lena is vulnerable; in general, the women in the orchestra are a commodity for their company as much as their music, with the implication that little distinction is made between their erotic and their musical desirability. Lena first meets Heyst, who has happened upon the orchestra (memorably described as "murdering silence with a vulgar, ferocious energy," 69) in his hotel as he ventures from his seclusion to conduct business with his bank. Heyst sympathizes with the women of the orchestra, "these beings exploited, hopeless, devoid of charm and grace and whose fate of cheerless dependence invested with a touch of pathos their coarse and joyless features" (70), offering a dire assessment of such women's lives given their lack of desirability and their utter dependence on men. Then, Heyst unexpectedly spots "a girl," assessing her form with wonder: "It was evident that she was a girl. It was evident in the outline of the shoulders, in the slender white bust springing up, rigid, and barred slantwise by the crimson sash, from the large bell-shaped spread of muslin skirt hiding the chair on which she sat averted a little from the body of the hall" (71). Conrad characterizes Heyst's increasing physical desire for Lena in their interactions as "heat," connecting it to his feelings of alienation as well as his compassion: "And though he had made up his mind to retire from the world in hermit fashion yet he was irrationally moved by this sense of loneliness which had come to him in the hour of renunciation. It hurt him. Nothing is more painful than the shock of sharp contradictions that lacerate our intelligence and our feelings" (86, 68). The son of a nihilist philosopher who looms large even in death, Heyst struggles to reconcile his innate compassion and altruistic tendencies with the alienated worldview he has inherited. Heyst acts impulsively as Lena becomes a means of alleviating the alienation that is requisite to living with his father's philosophy, yet this act also requires that Heyst find a way to live with Lena, whose mere presence challenges his solitude.

Immediately and true to form, Heyst longs not to take advantage of Lena's vulnerability, as the other men around her do, but to rescue her, an impulse that only grows as he comes to know her. In their first conversation, he "playfully" asks Lena to "command" him (73). With Heyst enraptured by her voice, Lena admits that she does not sing and alludes to her life, "I don't remember that I ever had much reason to sing since I was little" (74). As they get to know each other in the ensuing nights in concert intervals, she alludes to suicide "'And I am here,' she finished, 'with no one to care if I make a hole in the water the next chance I get or not" (77). In these public interactions in the concert hall, she describes her own desperation and alienation as a woman, particularly a woman consigned to this orchestra and subject to the machinations of its director. Suicide by drowning is, of course, the requisite end for the fallen woman in Victorian art and literature, and Lena thereby implies the hopelessness of her intractable situation in which her attractiveness serves her worse than the looks of the less appealing women of the orchestra.[2] Both Lena and Heyst enjoy their meetings, and Lena is used to being treated so poorly that Heyst's courtesy proves to be "exciting by its novelty alone" (77). So, Heyst offers to "steal" her away, acknowledging her status as a commodity to the orchestra and to the hotelkeeper who pursues her threateningly (78).

As Heyst conspires with her to escape, countering the other conspiracy against her, she must remind him of the threat posed by men's desire for her, since Heyst seems to be unaware: "You aren't like the others; you are like no one in the world I ever spoke to" (83). Heyst, surprised by his attraction to her, still does not treat her as a commodity. He seems unconcerned about her sexual past and unable to relate to the men who value her as both desirable and "fallen." Indeed, to some extent, Heyst seems to stand outside of the sexual marketplace and the valuations that have cost her so dearly. While his father's influence on Heyst has caused him to disdain relationships, an inheritance that disables him emotionally, his passion for Lena mingles with his fundamental decency and compassion. As their relationship develops, Conrad connects Heyst's desire to her need for his assistance, calling on melodramatic phrases and images to portray the progression of his passion for Lena: "he felt her

---

[2] See L.J. Nicoletti (2004, 2007) on the classic traits of Victorian female suicide, as referenced in the previous chapter.

clinging to him after the manner of supplicants the world over. [...] The heaving of her breast and the trembling of all her limbs, in the closeness of her embrace, seemed to enter his body, infect his very heart" (81). Her supplication clearly enhances his desire, as he longs to rescue her. In discussing *Chance*, Robert Hampson (1996) comments that Conrad "hints [...] that chivalric psychology actually finds erotic stimulation in the distress of the woman it presents itself as rescuing. The woman is thus positioned as victim in the script of chivalric desire" (144). Certainly, Conrad dramatizes Heyst's similarities to the other men who desire Lena, particularly Schomberg with his fantasies of Lena's reinvigorating his manhood, even as Conrad emphasizes Heyst's more humane sympathy.

As the story is revealed gradually in the recounted conversations that make up the first part of the novel, the threat against Lena is indeed alarming. The narrator repeats a conversation between Davidson and Schomberg, the hotelkeeper who pursued Lena: "He shot out an infamous word which made Davidson start. That's what the girl was; and he reiterated the assertion that she was nothing to him" (52). While Schomberg's characterization of Lena, presumably calling her a whore, seems simply like sour grapes once she has departed with Heyst, as discussed in the first chapter, Conrad uses Mrs. Schomberg as a double for Lena; she is the battered wife who helps Lena escape to protect her own unenviable position. Presumably Schomberg once desired his wife as well, but now she is described as "an It—[...] a very plain dummy, with an arrangement for bowing the head at times and smiling stupidly now and then," illustrating Lena's real jeopardy from Schomberg as well as a depicting a concise study of trauma in a case of domestic violence: "Though his eyes strayed about irresolutely yet his swollen angry features awakened in the miserable woman he had been tyrannizing for years a fear for his precious carcass; since the poor creature had nothing else to hold onto in the world" (46–47, 98–99). Once the bandits arrive to threaten and manipulate Schomberg, he defaults to a vision couched in the language of the adventure story, grasping at his melodramatic fantasy of Lena to counter his emasculation: "Ah, if only he had that girl with him he would have been masterful and resolute and fearless—fight twenty desperadoes—care for nobody on earth! Whereas the possession of Mrs. Schomberg was no incitement to a display of manly virtues. Instead of caring for no one, he felt he cared for nothing" (101). Thus, his alienation, crudely sketched in a few words, ironically comes to parallel Heyst's similar desolation on the island, but Schomberg's frustration manifests itself in the coarse desire for violence: "Sometimes he was tempted to screw that head [of his wife] off the stalk. He imagined himself doing it—with one hand, a twisting movement. Not seriously of course. Just a simple indulgence for his exasperated feelings. He wasn't capable of murder. He was certain of that"; then, the narration wryly adds that he was "... quite unaware that he had murdered the poor woman morally years ago" (109). Conrad sets the dark comedy of Schomberg's puffed-up fantasies of violence against his weakness and cowardice, an internal frustration that he easily displaces on to the wife he sees as the impediment to his gaining Lena in the first place.

Like the "exploited, hopeless" older women in Zangiacomo's orchestra, Mrs. Schomberg demonstrates another version of the fate of a woman, powerless and unprotected, in a society where men control commerce, including sexual commerce (70). The men view her with scorn and sympathy, but Davidson gradually evinces amazement: "As to Mrs. Schomberg, she sat there like a joss" (61). The narrator continues, "Davidson was lost in admiration. He believed now that the woman had been putting it on for years. She never even winked. It was immense! The insight he had obtained almost frightened him. [...] She was a miracle of dissimulation" (61). Of course, Conrad makes clear to the reader the abuse that has made such "dissimulation" essential, yet this depiction also recalls the familiar depiction of the conniving woman. If there is comedy in her very absurdity, the character of Mrs. Schomberg serves as another painful reminder of the failure of the Victorians' ideology of benevolent paternalism in practice, a deliberate and disturbing portrait of intimate violence.

This vision of a woman consumed or "used up" by the hard treatment of her husband or lover echoes the plot of another contemporary Conrad story and the life of a woman, "Laughing Anne," whose treatment and fate are arguably worse than Mrs. Schomberg's. Conrad (1924b) wrote the story "Because of the Dollars" (later dramatized and eventually filmed as *Laughing Anne*) while he was writing *Victory*, and it also features Captain Davidson, the sometime interlocutor of the narrator in *Victory*, but as a central character—more comparable to Heyst in *Victory*—whose own marriage fails because of his compassionate humanity in refusing to abandon a desperate woman and her son. Another character who resonates with Lena's experience and possible fate, Anne represents a familiar Victorian fallen woman narrative: She falls in love with "Pearler Harry," who is apparently her first lover, and, thus, the man whose attentions

transformed her into a "fallen" woman (*WT* 178). He "brought her out
first into these parts—from Australia, I believe [...] and then dropped
her, and she remained knocking about here and there" (178–179). She
goes from man to man, getting "dropped" each time after a year or two
despite her "pleasant silvery laugh," and falling to worse men for companionship as she tries to secure a life for her young son (179). Alluding
to sexual commerce, she tells Davidson she hopes to give up "paint and
dyes," a lost figure haunting a Malay settlement in a "fanciful tea-gown
thing, dingy pink satin, with a long train and frayed lace trimmings; her
eyes like black coals in a pasty-white face" (183, 181). Like Lena, Anne
dies tragically, protecting Davidson from bandits (though he is not her
lover, which departs from the aspects of the plot that parallel *Victory*), a
resonant, poignant rendering of a familiar trope. Despite her low status,
Anne holds on to her European identity, which makes her both distinct
from the Malay women in her shabby European gentility and identified
with them as Other in European culture because of her fallenness. As
Armstrong (1998) explains, nineteenth-century anthropological studies
associated "the desires of primitive people" with those they "had attributed to European prostitutes" (538). In "Because of the Dollars," the
narrator notes pointedly of Anne's last lover, Bamtz, who has sunk very
low, that still "he had always kept clear of native women," making it clear
that even the disgusting Bamtz would not choose a "native woman" as
a lover (180). Thus, as Armstrong comments, "The degraded double
of the ideal English woman ensures that the bond among men remains
a bond among family-minded men even when they are far away from
home" (558). Anne's grasping at a facsimile of the gentility that utterly
eludes her points up her degradation all the more; except for the generous Davidson, the men around her see her as spent, lacking the sexual
attractiveness that can be bartered for security, and she knows her days
using herself as a commodity to support her child are over.

Lena's situation, while not as desperate as Anne's, places her in a
similarly double position. When Captain Davidson initially discusses the
orchestra with Mrs. Schomberg trying to gain additional information
about his friend Heyst's departure, she gives him the crucial fact, "There
was even one English girl" who, she clarifies, is "[y]oung enough"
(72). Being slim, fair, youthful, and English, in this context, she initially represents the European "salon body" described by Armstrong as
the counterpart to the "colonial Other and the unideal woman" who
"were viewed as deviant, dark, disease-bearing, desiring, lacking in
self-control, and eminently readable" (Davis and Schleifer 1998, 536).

Lena is prized by Schomberg, by Zangiacomo the bandleader, and perhaps by Heyst because she recalls the pure European ideal even to her white performance dress, though she is not a "good girl" in her own estimation (171). Lena's sexuality is obscured somewhat in the novel; we know that she and Heyst become lovers on the island,[3] but it is not clear whether she has yet been a prostitute prior to their meeting or whether Zangiacomo has simply used her beauty and the possibility of her sexual availability to sell tickets. Lena occupies a kind of contested space in the novel; as a European, she contrasts the Malay women, and not being "the sort that men turn their backs on" she is not (yet) desperate in the way that Laughing Anne is (82). She is able to make choices to refuse Schomberg and to leave with Heyst, yet her sexuality marks her throughout the novel, Othering her in a way that links her to Malay women rather than Europeans, a version of Armstrong's image of the "double-bodied woman." Heyst's distrust of her "charm" and his desire for her causes him to suspect her fidelity even as she lies dying in his arms. Lena's youth, vulnerability, and appearance connect her with the European ideal woman at home to the European men in Malaysia. However, pointedly, the fate of Laughing Anne in "Because of the Dollars" looms as a cautionary tale for the fallen woman, and the fate of Mrs. Schomberg in *Victory* looms as a cautionary tale for the faithful wife. Conrad makes it clear that there are no good options for someone in Lena's position, whose life is defined by her desirability to men. Even as Lena seems to accept her new life on the island, she longs to tether Heyst to her by fulfilling a kind of scripted romance founded on her self-sacrifice for love that reproduces the constricting gender roles she appears to have escaped.

II

"[H]e may yet end by eating her," the narrator comments wryly to Davidson in their discussions, alluding humorously to cannibalism, a familiar Conradian image (used perhaps most pointedly in *Heart of Darkness* and *The Secret Agent*), while evoking Lena and Heyst's

---

[3] They clearly consummate their relationship despite Conrad's relative subtlety on the details of their involvement to avoid the censors. See Hampson's commentary in *Conrad's Secrets* (2012).

fundamental inequality as a couple and the way her desirability threatens his self-image and perhaps her well-being (50). Yet the notion of
consumption is not just a laughing matter here: Lena has already been
shown to be a marketable commodity, one in need of Heyst's theft of
her to allow her to assert some power over herself. Her departure almost
leads to violence in the contest between Zangiacomo and Schomberg to
recover her and presages the bandits' violence to come. Her desirability
to the European men in Malaysian presumably will diminish as she ages
(as with Mrs. Schomberg or with Anne in "Because of the Dollars"), and
she longs to establish an emotional bond with Heyst, one that supersedes
the market viability that has defined her since her father became ill. Lena
explains to Heyst: "But sometimes it seems to me that you can't love me
for myself, only for myself, as people do love each other when it is to be
forever" (190).

When Lena flees with him to his island retreat, Samburan, Heyst,
from principle and inclination, allows her autonomy, yet their relationship is fundamentally unequal. Initially, he "steals" her as an act of
protection, and she asks him to name her, departing from the names
(including the name Magdalen, an obvious allusion to her position as a
fallen woman and, particularly, one who seeks redemption, though she
was also known as Alma) that were hers previously. Their habitation on
the island, which is his domain and dwelling furnished with his inherited belongings and attended by his servant, must serve to establish
his dominance, and she remains a "girl" as he mocks his own place in
middle age. However, his greatest power in the relationship is his mistrust of human involvement and his fear of "depart[ing] from the part
of an unconcerned spectator," the remnant of the what is described as
the "wrecked philosophy" of his father (161); he is moved by her but is
uncertain of their relationship and perhaps suspicious of her, sometimes
plagued by a "mood of grim doubt" (161). Meanwhile, Lena powerfully
desires acknowledgement of his answering passion, which she views as a
kind of womanly validation, longing for marks of his unyielding affection
and passion.

As the adventure plot plays out, the thieves arrive on the island under
false pretenses. When the youthful, attractive bandit, Ricardo, sees and
desires her, Lena decides to mount her own campaign to save herself
and Heyst. Initially, Ricardo observes Lena, wearing a sarong knot-
ted above her bust and twisting up her hair with bare arms in the bed-
room in her dwelling with Heyst. Lena fled with only the possessions

that could be carried in Mrs. Schomberg's scarf, and her sarong, a possession of Heyst's that puts her in Malay garb, connects her to local rather than European women (unlike poor Anne in her frayed satin and train). Conrad describes the scene as a kind of tableau, a lovely image of a European woman in Malaysian clothing dressing her hair before the mirror, and Ricardo responds violently and impulsively to the desirable vision before him, trying to rape Lena. She fights him powerfully but silently, and he flees without harming her, thinking he has found a kindred spirit, a woman who matches his violent, ruthless determination. Susan Jones (1999) considers the scene:

> Conrad's narrator (and, by implication, his reader) enters into an ambiguous space in which the woman hovers between her private self and her public appearance. Ricardo's attempted rape accentuates the implied violation engendered in the act of watching. Since we also share Ricardo's (physical) point of view, Conrad unsettles the position of the reader as passive observer of events taking place in the text. (184)

In this intimate, vulnerable moment Ricardo sees her as a sexual object, much as the *femme fatale* in an adventure story might be to its reader. Jones notes the objectification of Lena in these parallel scenes in *Victory*: "When Heyst looks in the mirror, his action signifies the soul searching and self-contemplation of the hero; Lena's scene comments on her status, not as self-reflective woman, but as passive and tempting object" (184). Despite the gender difference in the way that these mirror scenes are portrayed, if we read Conrad's presentation of Lena as a critique of the traditional views of the fallen woman and the threat of women's sexuality, then we must assume that the uncomfortable identification with Ricardo in this scene allows the reader to glimpse the pitfall that Heyst will fall into later in the novel, the presumption of the "double-bodied woman" that, at base, represents the primitive, instinctual drives she inspires in men, endangering them and their autonomy, Lena's doubleness associated with the only power over men that she has ever possessed. Of course, Lena views the pretense of seducing Ricardo as the only way to save her lover, a purpose she romanticizes as anything but instinctual; for her, it is a direct representation of the self-sacrificing nature of her love. However, Lena's appropriation of the knife emphasizes the extent to which she has undermined such traditional categories altogether, assuming masculine power as she alludes to the threat of the emasculating *femme fatale*. In the end, Ricardo associates Lena with a stereotypical, desirable feminine role rather than seeing her with clear eyes—a shortsighted response that will lead to his demise, satisfyingly for the reader inclined to sympathize with Lena.

Ultimately, Lena is able to turn the burden of her desirability, her sexuality, into a weapon to save Heyst and sacrifice herself; she pretends to conspire with Ricardo so she can disarm him. Lena's ploy for Heyst's affection merely points up the way in which she has defined herself primarily in relation to a series of men: her father, the bandleader, the predatory men like Schomberg who desire her, and finally Heyst, whose tenderness and compassion she misreads for the possibility of a kind of purifying passion. Her manipulation of Ricardo's desires and fantasies about her, playing into the Edenic sexuality of her co-habitation with Heyst and the sexual double standard for women, nearly alienates Heyst rather than binding him to her. For all of his compassion and intellectual distance, after her final fight with Ricardo, Heyst initially judges her as sexually base, capable of manipulating him as well as Ricardo. Heyst's overt, bitter reference to womankind's role in the fall (speaking to his Magdalen) as he recalls that "other attitude, suggestive of shame [which] had its charm" recalls the stereotyped Victorian portrayal of the threat of the sexualized woman, as sympathy for the plight of the fallen maid or the prostitute is tempered with disgust for her sexual knowledge and the desires she represents (345). Earlier, when Heyst asks Lena if she offered a prayer when she was "cornered" before Heyst rescued her, she replies "I am not what they call a good girl," again marking the irrevocable sexual standard (171). As any good Victorian knows, "fallen" women who have sex outside of marriage are not the sort deserve to have their prayers answered as hers have been in Heyst; instead, they make "a hole in the water" as she had contemplated (77).

It is his realization that Lena is injured that finally causes Heyst to abandon his judgment of her and react to her with instinct and compassion again. When Heyst realizes that Lena may be wounded, he immediately disrobes her to examine her flesh for wounds in front of Davidson, the captain trying to rescue Heyst, his crude judgment of her sexuality immediately cast aside. Conrad casts this scene as an ironic re-envisioning of a scene of sexual passion or violation: "as if possessed with a sudden fury, [Heyst] started tearing open the front of the girl's dress. She remained insensible under his hands, and Heyst let out a groan," but the groan is not the culmination of desire but "the heavy plaint of a man who falls, clubbed in the dark" (346). Lena's death did indeed fulfill Heyst's desire to be left alone in the image of his father and not to be subject to his emotions; and, yet, in typical Conradian irony, it is only through her death that he realizes his desire to be intimate with another person to relieve his profound solitude. Heyst can transcend neither his father's "wrecked philosophy" nor his hidden fears about the danger presented by female sexuality until it is too late and no semblance of their Edenic idyll can be recovered.

Lena lays claim to Heyst by her sacrifice, acknowledging that she has finally been able to use her sexuality as a weapon as Heyst intimates, though not in the spirit in which he portrays it, rather than be a victim of her desirability to men. She reclaims Ricardo's knife, which she had taken from him to protect Heyst, as "the symbol of her victory," one that represents her autonomy among the conflicted men (346). If Heyst has been "unmanned" by her passion for him and the force of his own response, Lena has taken on the masculine role in outmaneuvering the bandit. Even as she is dying in front of him, he remains guarded, "cursing his fastidious soul which even at that moment kept the true cry of love from his lips in its infernal mistrust of all" (347). As she exults, in prose studded with the overblown language of the popular romances that, presumably, have influenced her—"the sanctuary of her innermost heart," "the flush of rapture flooding her whole being," "with that divine radiance on her lips" (347)—Heyst begins to play his role in her script, all the while preparing himself for his own tragic role. No longer scapegoating Lena, Heyst reclaims his manhood in the ritual sacrifice he makes as he follows Lena's example in giving her life for a romantic ideal. In closing, Conrad offers Davidson's matter-of-fact rendering of Heyst's end as an eyewitness to the conflagration: "I suppose he couldn't stand his thoughts before her dead body—and fire purifies everything" (349).

Obviously, Conrad's ironic, self-conscious treatment of the trite aspects of this melodrama, even as he works to attain a critical distance for the reader through the complex narration, allows the reader to enjoy the expected formulaic, sentimental tragedy, while forcing the reader to consider the deeper social ramifications of the entrenched gender roles depicted here. If we can consider Lena's final sacrifice triumphantly as she does, taking possession of her femininity and the sexuality that has stood for victimization—prior to her relationship with Heyst anyway—to gain the acclaim she so desires, then she has finally rid herself of the burden of her sexuality to be judged on her own terms. Yet, ironically, she dies playing a role in a kind of artificial, scripted romance she has enacted, not free from the constraints which originally caused her to flee, but still trying to live up to the idealized representations of femininity she has internalized.

III

The central narrative of *The Arrow of Gold* begins appropriately in the transitory, festive chaos of Marseilles at Carnival, and our hero, holding himself aloof from the celebration becomes entranced by a masked young woman portraying Night among the Pierrots and Pierrettes: "the Night noticed perhaps my fixed gaze and throwing her body forward out of the wriggling chain shot out at me a slender tongue like a pink dart" (Conrad 1924a, 9). George is too surprised to react to her, but watches admiringly as the next man she approaches, sticking out her tongue, smiles and "chuck[s] her under the chin" (9). The narrative uses George's inability to respond to the playful act and join in the pleasurable provocations of Carnival to demonstrate his sexual inexperience and way in which his prior expectations about women confine him. Described several times in the novel as "stupid" and young, George, like Lena, embraces scripted gender roles from the beginning, remaining blinded to the reality of the seemingly legendary woman he desires, a woman clearly damaged—socially as well as psychologically in Conrad's rendering of her past abuse—by the absurdity of traditional gender roles and the way they reinforce men's desire to possess women as objects. Conrad addresses men's objectification of women, specifically in the figure of the fallen woman, unambiguously and repeatedly in the novel.

The Arrow of Gold's bracketed narratives and notes start by situating the gunrunner who will take the pseudonym of M. George as an innocent, manipulated by Mills and Captain Blunt during Carnival to assist the Carlist cause, which would return the Pretender, Don Carlos, to the Spanish throne. Mills and Blunt appeal to George via the trappings of romance: "A man who 'lived by the sword,' before my eyes, close at my elbow! Such people did exist in the world yet! I had not been born too late" (15). Another member of the Carlist group, Doña Rita de Lastaola, is openly admired and reviled as a kind of living decorative object, the model discovered in her childhood by a famous painter and known to be his mistress. Before George meets Rita, he is influenced by the other men's admiration for her; by the complexities of how they relate to her sexuality; and by the connection Blunt posits between the "amazing decapitated, mutilated dummy of a woman," a kind of mannequin that inhabits the room in which they discourse through the night, and the lovely, fallen Rita (122).

Thus, Conrad situates Rita in a complex web of male attitudes from the beginning of the novel. In its initial scenes, for both George and for the reader, the character of Rita is composed entirely of men's visions of her, which conflate her with the damaged, headless "articulated" dummy that was made to her measurements and sometimes stood in for her as an artist's model (21). Conrad's use of such a dramatic, overdetermined representation for Rita highlights from the beginning the absurdity and artificiality of Rita's relationships with men, as they project their desires and fantasies onto her elusive and highly prized form. While Rita's attractiveness is unquestionable, the "dummy" image recalls *Victory*'s Mrs. Schomberg, so damaged by her husband's abuse that she can do nothing but cling to her wifely role; once she loses her attractiveness, she can no longer compete on the marital or sexual market, and she has no other options for survival. Rita, too, suffers at the hands of her abusive cousin, as well as her strict uncle and sister and the array of men who long to seduce her. Not only is Rita desirable in her person, she inherited the artist Henry Allègre's immense wealth, and throughout the novel she longs for friendship that is not based these attributes and the roles associated with them that she performs.

Indeed, Rita is such a commodity that she remains isolated from genuine fellowship and companionship in her dealings with men; and the public nature of her past relationship with Allègre means she is unable to find friendship with, or even be received by, women. Even the restrained Mills comments, "I am not an easy enthusiast where women are concerned, but she was without doubt the most admirable find of his amongst all the priceless items he had accumulated in that house—the most admirable" (23), to which Blunt replies sarcastically, "But, you see, of all of the objects there she was the only one that was alive" (23). The novel returns to the possessiveness of various sorts of men in relation to Rita, while portraying it with an ironic distance that allows the reader to critique the stereotypical views they represent.

Rita's relationships with men repeatedly play out different versions of patriarchal domination. In her childhood, she is depicted as a barefoot, unself-conscious goatherd, the rustic opposite of her elegant adult self, whose girlhood "rusty" hair has yet to develop into the "tawny"

Pre-Raphaelite beauty of her adulthood.[4] George tells her dreamily: "You give one, with a perpetual and intense freshness, feelings and sensations that are as old as the world itself, and you imagine that your enchantment can be broken off anywhere, at any time! But it can't be broken" (223), evoking the image of Rita as enchantress that is repeated throughout the text. George describes for the reader his aesthetic response to Rita after their discussion about Blunt and his ill-fated proposal to Rita: "For the last two days my being was no longer composed of memories, but exclusively of sensations of the most absorbing, disturbing, exhausting nature. I was like a man who has been buffeted by the sea or by a mob till he loses all hold on the world in the misery of his helplessness" (221). Clearly, George relishes his initiation into this experience of passion and desire, wallowing in the overwhelming sensation that makes him, at least in his perception, pleasurably subject to a kind of dominating vision of Rita.

Rita's own initiation into her sexuality comes through a series of dominating and abusive encounters with her cousin (later disclosed to be Ortega) in her peasant girlhood. In their childhood, Ortega longs to dominate Rita, and repeatedly threatens to physically abuse her, bruising her in his frenzied interaction with her. His rage appears to be attributable to a kind of controlling desire that Rita does not reciprocate; Ortega's passion for her and his helplessness in the face of it seem to anger him. She has to hide herself to avoid the curses and threats of his passion, which are intermingled with proposals of marriage and avowals extracted under threat. While initially her descriptions seem to indicate primarily mental abuse and some physical violence by Ortega in their encounters, Rita's later disclosures might imply sexual violence or assault in their childhood encounters: "Rita's response to the threat represented by her cousin was to dissociate herself from her body" becoming corpse-like (Hampson 1996, 261). When she shows her sister, Therese, the bruises resulting from her encounters with Ortega, Therese turns

---

[4]Conrad uses language very close to Pater's language in *The Renaissance* to describe her mythic beauty, which at times echoes his famous reading of *La Gioconda*, yet he seems to be using it to evoke the sensations and sentiments of the innocent George, a youth of the kind who might have been affected by Pater's prose, which is roughly contemporary with the setting of the novel. See Bickley and Hampson (1998)(89).

on Rita, calling her "a sinful girl, a shameless creature," as though she invited Ortega's desire and abuse (113). Her fear of going out horseback riding alone as an independent, adult woman puzzles George and Mills, but we later learn that Rita knows the possessive and obsessive Ortega has been following her social and political life. She fears both his humiliating interventions, the resurgence of a past from which she has irrevocably distanced herself, and his possessive violence towards her, an attitude which George later describes as "Mine—or Dead" (310).

When Henry Allègre "discovers" Rita as a teenager, her innocence of the important social worlds into which the artist promenades her places her into a situation of incredible isolation. Her sexual relationship with him means she cannot be received by women in society, and, thus, she has no women friends. The men of Allègre's circle treat her reverently as an art object, salaciously as a sexually available woman, or as some problematic combination of the two. Allègre both shields her and sacrifices her, indulging through her his desire to reject traditional social mores, discomfiting his friends and acquaintances by forcing them to deal with his young, beautiful model and mistress openly: "To lift a girl out of the tide of common things at a moment when she has awakened to caprice and passion and to convert physical enchantment into a semblance of plastic art with the power to arouse and then to repel desire is Allègre's expression of the aesthete's scorn for the natural, an *épater le bourgeois* joke" (Wiley 1966, 165). Allègre made Rita his heiress, leaving her wealthy, but left her to navigate the brutal social world of late-century Europe without his protection, a figure for the fallen woman, both desirable and shameful, in his social set.

Rita's self-possession and confidence in her own worth seem remarkable given her peasant past and her surroundings, as though she's trying to find a way to exist without shame in a society that has yet to comprehend her autonomy. Rita later refuses the proposal of Captain Blunt, since his genuine affection for her is infused with disdainful desire:

> He believes in a soul the same way that Therese does, as something that can be touched with grace or go to perdition; and he doesn't want to be damned with me before his own judgment seat. He is a most noble and loyal gentleman, but I have my own Basque peasant soul and don't want to think that every time he goes away from my feet—yes, *mon cher*, on this carpet, look for the marks of scorching—that he goes away feeling tempted to brush the dust off his moral sleeve. That! Never! (*AG* 209)

Here and elsewhere, Conrad posits a clear-eyed Rita, a woman who has not bought into the sexual double standard that disparages her for her sexual relationships any more than the prejudice against the class from which she was elevated. She implies she believes in a soul in a different way than Blunt and Therese, whose judgments condemn her for impurity. Remarkably, she does not seem to be ill at ease with who she is, though she must constantly be on guard against the very men who surround, assist, and befriend her. Conrad counters those who would call Rita a fallen woman or a "catin," a whore, as Ortega does, with what seems to be a deliberate allusion to the figure of the New Woman, formidable, astute, and unashamed of her sexuality. Rita constitutes herself as a mature woman in her description of her response to Blunt's proposal:

I didn't spare him. I told him plainly that to want a woman formed in mind and body, mistress of herself, free in her choice, independent in her thoughts; to love her apparently for what she is and at the same time to demand from her the candour and the innocence that could only be a shocking pretence; to know her such as life had made her and at the same to despise her secretly for every touch with which her life had fashioned her—that was neither generous nor high minded; it was positively frantic. (211)

Rita characterizes her sexuality and her relationships as part of her education, "such as life had made her," and refuses to pretend innocence, absurdly, as she notes, to satisfy his pretensions, commenting wryly, "He must have felt like a man who betrayed himself for nothing" (213). The reader might recall Hardy's description of Tess's early life, particularly her sexual life: "But for the world's opinion those experiences would have been simply a liberal education" (117), an obvious critique of the double standard and one which alludes to Tess's story as a kind of *Bildungsroman*. Rita acknowledges her sexuality as a crucial part of her maturation, but she refuses to make sexual purity—or the lack thereof— her defining trait, acknowledging her path to adulthood to George, as he pursues his own sentimental education.

Rita repudiates the judgment of Blunt and, by extension, Therese and Ortega, asking, "could I have rushed away from him to shut myself in a convent? Could I? After all I have a right to my share of daylight" (213). This notion of a "share of daylight" recalls Susan Bacadou's appeal in Conrad's story "The Idiots" (addressed in the second chapter) in the final moments before her death: "I want to live. To live alone—for a week—for a day. I must explain to them" (*TU* 84). Each woman makes a plea for independence, to be able to depart from constricting social judgments associated with femininity (of course, Susan's crime, though committed in self-defense against her husband's intended rape, precludes any such freedom). Rita can think more freely, commenting to George, "Yet for the most part [men can only dominate women] because women choose more or less consciously to let them do so" (215), a statement that implies the personal and social stakes of a refusal to be dominated, since, as the novel demonstrates, women, as well as men, socialize women and girls to comply with traditional gender roles and have a stake in their perpetuation.[5]

DeKoven (1999) describes the New Woman of the turn of the century as "independent, educated, (relatively) sexually liberated, oriented more toward productive life in the public sphere than toward reproductive life in the home" (174). In *The Secret Agent*, Conrad alludes to the figure of New Woman in the character Winnie Verloc; in the novel's final scenes, she is characterized repeatedly and ironically as "the free woman" after Stevie's death and her murder of her husband.[6] Yet Winnie does not know how to live on her own without a man to define her. Conrad implies that her marriage has functioned as a kind of prostitution ("seven years of security for Stevie loyally paid for on her part," 220) from which she transitions in her desperation, shocking herself by offering herself sexually to Ossipon without marriage in the effort to regain the security and protection of a man on any terms once her husband is dead. In contrast to her lack of physical passion for her husband, at least Winnie finds Ossipon attractive, but he abandons her soon after he discovers her appalling crime. Despite the implicit critiques of patriarchal culture in *The Secret Agent*, there is no place for a New Woman in the novel, and Winnie cannot imagine such a life for herself on her own. Yet the character of Rita in *The Arrow of Gold*—mistreated and objectified by men so often in her life, and excluded from the society of women—offers a clear

---

[5] See Elizabeth Langland's discussion of women's investment in traditional gender ideology in *Nobody's Angels: Middle-Class Women and Domestic Ideology in Victorian Culture* (1995).

[6] I consider the portrayal of Winnie in relation to the figure of the New Woman in more detail in "The Female Offender, the New Woman, and Winnie Verloc in *The Secret Agent*" (Harrington 2007).

valorization of her adult, independent, desiring, and experienced self, an understanding of herself as autonomous, that Winnie is certainly incapable of articulating and perhaps even grasping. While Rita is depicted as a kind of Pre-Raphaelite enchantress on the exterior, the glimpses we get of her inner life recall an empowered modern woman and critique the absurdity of infantilizing or objectifying an individual in whom we can discern a complex inner life.

IV

In its opening chapters, *The Arrow of Gold* establishes Rita as George's seducer for the Carlist cause, the historical frame for the novel in the 1880s: "It was Doña Rita who would have to do the persuading; for, after all, such an enterprise with its ugly and desperate risks was not a trifle to put before a man—however young" (6). The narration makes it clear that George was set up deliberately: Mills "might even have envied" George's nature and George waits urgently for Mills to appear, ironically performing the role of suitor for Mills, yet George is also described as Mills's "victim" (6). The story, framed in part by Carnival celebrations in Marseilles, deliberately evokes the *Bildungsroman*, as George offers a wiser (if limited) perspective on youthful experiences: "If anything, it is perhaps a little sympathy that the writer expects for his buried youth" (*AG* 4). Daphna Erdinast-Vulcan (1988) highlights Conrad's self-conscious evocation of archetypes in *The Arrow of Gold*: "Both [George] and Rita are possessed by a sense of their own unreality: both seem to suspect that their own existence is predicated upon a fictional—and fictitious—model" (219). Certainly, the novel deliberately foregrounds the act of representation, especially the ways in which fictionalized representations can shape the way individuals relate to each other.

Like the other men in the narrative, George is intrigued by Rita's connection to the dummy, the stand-in that was "made to measure" for Rita's body: "After taking possession of the studio I had raised it tenderly, dusted its mangled limbs and insensible, hard-wood bosom, and then had it propped up in a corner where it seemed to take on, of itself, a shy attitude" (240). Not only does George treat the damaged doll "tenderly," though it also resembles Rita figuratively in its "insensible, hard-wood bosom," but he projects "a shy attitude" onto it. Conrad emphasizes the weird intimacy of men with this dummy throughout the narrative: it functions as a sexualized object, invested with Rita and horribly mutilated as a counterpoint to her beauty. George considers its relationship to Rita as "a faint, miserable illusion of the original, less arti-ficial than a photograph, less precise, too" (241). While the damage to the dummy clearly alludes to Rita's interior trauma, it also represents a disturbing image of men's desire to essentialize Rita and brutalize her, figuratively or otherwise, to regain control of their own passions.

As noted, Rita has "the physical appearance of a Pre-Raphaelite model—in particular the auburn hair and full mouth," and her portrayal echoes the Pre-Raphaelites, since "[f]or much of the novel, indeed, Rita is an image rather than a woman" (Bickley and Hampson 1988, 84, 88). Roberts explores the competing desires at play in the image of Rita:

> The idea of Rita as unique yet universal is repeatedly expressed in the novel by a formulation invented by Allègre, but repeated by other of the men: the description of Rita as "the woman of all time". [...] The implication of this dubious compliment, apart from denying that Rita is an ordinary person with human needs, is to make her infinitely scarce, infinitely to be competed for, a "priceless" commodity according to the economic laws of the market, here transposed to the psychological principles of a male sexual economy. (544)

Indeed, Rita is powerfully aware of the markets she must navigate, and the loneliness of being perceived as a commodity, one who reflects men's desires back to them rather than someone with her own "human needs." Through these attributes, Conrad portrays her as a kind of feminine archetype: young, strikingly lovely, and wealthy, yet sexually knowledge-able and "fallen," and thus confined to the society of men. As in *Victory*, Conrad seems to be considering the ramifications of what Armstrong will describe as the double-bodied woman; Rita's circumscribed role of the *femme fatale* is questioned continually in the narrative, which emphasizes Rita's alienated position in relation to the men who surround her and the absurdity of their views of her. She describes them as "ugly toads" in "boxes," an apt metaphor for the sexual politics she must navigate that humorously inverts their perception of her, making her the collector rather than the *objet d'art* (100).

The seductive vision of supposedly subversive politics in the novel's portrayal of Carlism, the adventuresome opportunity to make a reputa-tion as a gunrunner, and the "fallen" desirability of the Rita (for whom most men's admiration is always tinged with scorn) entice George, whose naïveté about Rita is striking given the reputation he establishes with the Carlists. Yet, George, who does not share Blunt's disgust at her sexuality, still cannot establish an understanding of Rita apart from his fawning, amorous fantasy of her, despite her desire to establish a friendship on different terms. The novel recounts several instances of miscommunication between Rita and George in which she opens up to him, attempting to share her fears and struggles, but he is unable to relate to her outside of his own awe-struck desire; thus, he cannot fully acknowledge or assimilate the complexity of her character. His youthful naiveté contrasts positively with Blunt's perverse mixture of condescension and desire, which links sophistication to cruelty, yet George's marked imperceptiveness is similarly perverse. Roberts (1992), in his thoughtful reading of gender in the novel, remarks on "the cruelty of an insistence on an aesthetic/idealizing response to someone who desperately needs, as Rose seeks to remind George, a 'friend'—that is, who needs someone to treat her as a person, with ordinary feelings, weaknesses, strengths, desires, needs, not as a statue, in ideal, an embodiment of a supposed female principle, or as a 'catin'" (547). While George does not judge Rita for her sexuality as most of the other men do, he remains dedicated to scripting a role for her that posits worshipful admiration rather than cordial, or even intimate, understanding, willfully blind to her desire to be honest with him.

Jones (1999) notes Conrad's deliberate inversion in the description of George's version of the female toilet in one scene as George brushes his hair before the mirror, longing for Rita, and "seeking her (absent) gaze to complete his sense of identity. Yet as with the example of Heyst in *Victory*, the reversal of gender roles does not necessarily imply the emasculation of the hero, rather the questioning of romance codes that fix the female in a conventionally passive position" (185). Certainly, Rita's characteristic view of herself supports the notion that Conrad envisions a woman who is hampered by the ideals others foist on her, the possibility of a different understanding of Rita that lurks below the superficial view of her, as well as, Jones implies, a more complex gendering of characters than is typical of conventional romance. As Bickley and Hampson (1988) comment, George's "perception of Rita catches precisely that combination of beauty and elusiveness characteristic of Rossetti's portraits of women" (85). This tendency to incorporate Rita into a kind of "elusive" and mythic femininity on George's part (which the novel both participates in and critiques) comments on the way in which popular representations and the romance codes that inform them can reduce women to emblems, characterized by monolithic considerations of women's sexuality.

The plot involving Rita comes to a climax involving Ortega's violent obsession with her, the almost absurd restaging of a kind of primal sexual scene from her childhood. George brings Ortega, who is acting for the Carlists, to safe haven in one of Rita's properties, after George discovers Ortega's identity and that George needs to protect Rita from Ortega's machinations against her. When he unexpectedly encounters Rita privately in one of the other rooms, George tries to gain resolution regarding their own relationship by speaking with her: "The tie between us is broken. I don't know that it was ever close. It was an external thing" (290). When he evinces distress over having had to sink his vessel under threat, she consoles him kindly and condescendingly that the love of his boat "was a safe love for you" (291). Yet each time he tries to approach her, to be consoled or embraced by her, she does not respond. When he remarks on her coldness like "granite" (resembling the sculptures for which she sat), she replies conventionally, "Nothing would be easier than to die for you," and he criticizes her "charlatanism of passion": "What has it got to do between you and me who are the only two beings in the world that may safely say that we have no need for shams between ourselves?" (299). Though George reasonably asks for an honest understanding between them, he is still in the grip of his own disorienting desire for her, and the narrative again casts him as a youthful aesthete having a sublime experience of Rita's beauty and desirability: "Man is a strange animal. [...] All I wanted was to keep her in her pose, excited and still, sitting up with her hair loose, softly glowing, the dark brown fur making a wonderful contrast with the white lace on her breast. [...] I cared for nothing but that sublimely aesthetic impression. [...] It had a divine strain. I am certain I was not in my right mind" (304). As he objectifies Rita, George's aestheticized passion is contrasted with the disturbing, violent passion of Ortega; keeping "her in her pose" recalls her doubling with the dummy all too clearly. While George means well as he tries to assist Rita, he has fallen into a reverie at a crucial moment in Ortega's plot, and he struggles to relate to her as a person rather than an object of contemplation.

Once Ortega realizes Rita is present, he calls out to her desperately in terms of passion and insult: "beloved," "beast," and *"Catin! Catin! Catin!"* even claiming that Rita has been a whore "from the cradle"

(320, 321). Rita's response to Ortega is an extreme version of her habitual coldness with regard to men, something approaching physical shock. When George speaks to her about Ortega, she replies, "I have a horror of myself. All true. All true" (333). Her belief in her own autonomy and rectitude is shaken by this voice from her childhood, recalling the past abuse she suffered. Ortega blames Rita for his passion, as though she had been a seducer in her girlhood, and longs to possess her and to kill her, a Browningesque villain who comically injures himself trying to use as a weapon an "Abyssinian or Nubian production of a bizarre shape," collected by Allègre as a curiosity, to break into the room (325). It is easy for the reader to dismiss Ortega as an absurd adversary, yet his character effectively represents the damaging patriarchalism that has followed Rita from her early life and that prevents Rita from living the unfettered life of a character like George, whose Carlist gunrunning represents autonomy and adventure envied by Rita. Like Lena, Rita seems to long for a kind of impossible freedom that men in the narrative take for granted.

Once Ortega is disarmed and convalescing, Rita and George acknowledge their mutual feelings and flee together to a "precarious bliss" in the "region of the Maritime Alps" (337, 338). When Ortega calls Rita "Catin!" like a vision from the archaic Victorian past, he represents that sexual judgment of women, present in Blunt and Therese as well, that Rita and George are able to ultimately refute so she can to have a relationship with George and come to terms with her past, albeit in a distant refuge with him. Hampson (1992) argues that this interlude represents a progression in their mutual understanding: "In *The Arrow of Gold*, the narrative presents not a journey within the self of the narrator, but rather the establishment of a precarious interdependence between its two central figures, the mature mutuality that Heyst and Lena failed to achieve in *Victory*" (270–271). This possibility of a "mature mutuality" is implied in the text, yet the reader must take it somewhat skeptically. The narrator of this "Second Note," which concludes the novel, remarks that they express themselves with "unreserve" in their cohabitation, but mentions the possibility of Rita's playing a part—or at least knowing that their Edenic refuge could not endure: "But if in this she was a comedienne then it was but a great achievement of her ineradicable honesty. Having once renounced her honorable scruples she took good care that he should taste no flavour of misgivings in the cup" (338). In this interlude, the narrative returns figuratively to the image of Carnival from early in the novel, a time of fleeting pleasure. That refusal to allow George to taste the "flavour of misgivings" signals that Rita is again playing a role, assuming a disguise that flatters George's idea of their relationship. After George returns to Marseilles on business and is injured in a duel with Blunt on her behalf, Rita nurses him back to health, then mysteriously departs, never to return to him or even to be found by her old acquaintance. Like the young girl disguised as Night provocatively sticking out her tongue, Rita can masquerade seductively for George, but this role is not one that she can sustain.

Roberts (1992) reads her affair with George as a kind of compromise: "Rita has decided to act out George's fantasy as a temporary refuge. This is not to deny that she might have been happy, since there can be a pleasure in being what someone else wants you to be, and it is what she has been trained for all her life. But she knows too much to keep it up indefinitely—knows that it would be the real death of her self" (532). In *The Arrow of Gold*, Rita's character is portrayed only in glimpses in the unreliable narration of M. George and the speculative narration of the writer of the two notes that enclose the text, yet Conrad clearly invites us to view her flight as an escape, if one that the deluded George cannot assimilate into his adoring view of her.

She leaves, presumably, so that she ceases to be defined by men and her own outsize persona. It would seem that Rita must leave fashionable society to be fully in possession of herself, to control her identity and sexuality without judgment. As Madame Léonore comments sagely, early in the narrative, "She is for no man! She would be vanishing out of their hands like water that cannot be held" (135). Indeed, Conrad exposes the image of Rita as mere illusion, a mirror for men's desires in the novel, highlighting men's ambivalence towards Rita as an independent woman through a series of often archetypal feminine images foisted upon Rita that are made to seem deliberately absurd in the process: "old enchantress"; "catin" or whore; mistress; adventuress; art object; and, of course, the mutilated dummy. To some extent, all of the men surrounding Rita in the narrative (except perhaps Mills, whose view of her is enigmatic) seem to espouse antiquated, sentimentalized, and sometimes chivalric views of women in Rita that fail to comprehend her character. Rita here serves as a representation of the persistent sexual double standard that Conrad, with his characteristic irony, holds up for critique. In *The Arrow of Gold*, Conrad borrows the popular proverb from Boccaccio that "lips that have been kissed do not lose their freshness" with regard to

Rita,[7] demonstrating the way in which her sexual experience both enhances Rita's value and decimates it in the eyes of others. She does not possess, or even value, the purity that underlies traditional, gendered social strictures.

Despite George's professional success, maturation, and the understanding he achieves as he comes to know Rita, he cannot release her from his script, even after she departs: "The self-conscious attitude of the protagonist and his doubts about his own identity make for a narrative that oscillates between a passionate affirmation of the code of romance upon which the protagonist's assumed identity is modeled, and a skeptical attitude, punctuated by self-inflicted stabs of irony, which deflate the rhetoric of passion" (Erdinast-Vulcan 1988, 219–220). Conrad invites the reader to view Rita outside of George's romance as neither his damsel in distress nor the "catin" that the men who surround her see, self-consciously treating the elements of romance in the text as attributes of genre, incorporated with elements of the adventure story, the mystery, the *Bildungsroman*. In concluding the novel with Rita as a figure for the elusive feminine, an object of longing that can never be fully possessed to satiate desire, Conrad invites the reader to consider the fuller individual outside of the limited frame; Rita's pleas for genuine understanding and friendship and her confident sense of self—and of her worth—despite the threatening and illicit qualities applied to her sexuality by Blunt, Ortega, and others, critique the sexual economy they represent. Despite Conrad's satirizing of the feminist Mrs. Fyne in *Chance* and likely antipathy towards popular representations of the New Woman,[8] *The Arrow of Gold* struggles with precisely the issues that are at stake for the turn-of-the-nineteenth-century feminism. As Roberts (1992) maintains, the novel is not a "sustained, powerful and deliberate feminist critique," but it bears a relationship to feminist critique elsewhere in Conrad's later work (532). The value of *The Arrow of Gold* as a critique of patriarchy lies in the way it takes up the depiction of women, the illusions surrounding gender identity, allowing those glimpses of Rita that are less filtered by George's emotions to depict a woman in direct conflict with the absurdly circumscribed roles she apparently occupies.

---

[7] See Bickley and Hampson's excellent consideration of this source in "'Lips that have been kissed': Boccaccio, Verdi, and *The Arrow of Gold*" (1988).

[8] See Susan Jones's discussion in *Conrad and Women* (1999), particularly pages 101–102.

George's maturation offers him no better perspective on Rita, much as Heyst's realizations in *Victory* come too late. Hampson (1992) views *The Arrow of Gold* as a successful rendering of what Conrad only attempted to achieve in *Victory:* "the merging of psychological realism with mythic and symbolic modes, and the use of melodrama for the purposes of deeper psychological analysis" (271). Again, melodrama and those expectations in terms of gender and genre that it generates become the vehicle for a critique of broader gender constraints and the way it distorts relationships between individuals. Considering DeKoven's (1999) definition of modernism as a movement whose "masculinist misogyny, however, was almost universally accompanied by its dialectical twin: a fascination and strong identification with the empowered feminine" (174), these novels can be seen to frame the problem of women's sexuality in terms of men's struggle to adjust to women's empowerment in a world where female sexual purity is ceasing to be the dominant valuation. *Victory* and *The Arrow of Gold* end with an acknowledgment of the profound loss represented by the self-sacrifice of one woman and the deliberate disappearance of the other. However, in having Heyst come to some realization about his own ideological limitations, even if it leads only to his suicide, and in having Rita flee to start a new life outside of her web of suitors, lovers, and Carlist intrigues, the novels offer a glimpse of self-recognition on the part of these characters, even if it remains a possibility that cannot be envisioned further in the text.

REFERENCES

Acton, William. (1857) 1999. "Prostitution." In *Victorian Prose,* ed. Rosemary J. Mundhenk and LuAnn McCracken Fletcher, 221–227. New York: Columbia University Press.
Armstrong, Nancy. 1998. "The Occidental Alice." In *Contemporary Literary Criticism: Literary and Cultural Studies,* ed. Robert Davis and Ronald Schleifer, 536–563. New York : Longman.
Bickley, Pamela and Robert Hampson. 1988. "'Lips That Have Been Kissed': Boccaccio, Verdi, Rossetti and *The Arrow of Gold.*" *L'Epoque Conradienne,* 77–91.
Conrad, Joseph. 1924a. *The Arrow of Gold: A Story between Two Notes.* New York: Doubleday, Page, and Company.
———. 1924b. "Because of the Dollars." In *Within the Tides,* 169–211. Garden City, NY: Doubleday, Page, and Company.

———. 1924c. "The Idiots." In *Tales of Unrest*, 93–142. Garden City, NY: Doubleday, Page, and Company.
———. 1924d. *The Secret Agent: A Simple Tale*. Garden City, NY: Doubleday, Page, and Company.
———. 2016. *Victory: An Island Tale*, ed. J.H. Stape and Alexandre Fachard. Cambridge: Cambridge University Press.
Davis, Robert and Ronald Schleifer. 1998. Introduction. "The Occidental Alice." By Nancy Armstrong. In *Contemporary Literary Criticism: Literary and Cultural Studies*, ed. Robert Davis and Ronald Schleifer, 536–537. New York: Longman.
DeKoven, Marianne. 1991. *Rich and Strange: Gender, History, Modernism*. Princeton: Princeton University Press.
———. 1999. "Modernism and Gender." In *The Cambridge Companion to Modernism*, ed. Michael Levenson, 174–193. Cambridge: Cambridge University Press.
Erdinast-Vulcan, Daphna. 1988. "Conrad's Double-Edged Arrow." *Conradiana* 20 (3): 215–228.
Graham, Kenneth. 1996. "Conrad and Modernism." In *The Cambridge Companion to Joseph Conrad*, ed. J.H. Stape, 203–222. Cambridg: Cambridge University Press.
Hampson, Robert. 1992. *Joseph Conrad: Betrayal and Identity*. New York: St. Martin's Press.
———. 1996. "The Late Novels." *The Cambridge Companion to Joseph Conrad*, ed. J. H. Stape, 140–159. Cambridge: Cambridge University Press.
———. 2012. *Conrad's Secrets*. Basingstoke, UK: Palgrave Macmillan.
Hardy, Thomas. (1892) 1998. *Tess of the d'Urbervilles*, ed. John Paul Riquelme. Boston: Bedford/St. Martin's.
Harrington, Ellen Burton. 2007. "The Female Offender, the New Woman, and Winnie Verloc in *The Secret Agent*." *The Conradian* 32 (1): 57–69.
Jones, Susan. 1999. *Conrad and Women*. Oxford: Oxford University Press.
Langland, Elizabeth. 1995. *Nobody's Angels: Middle-Class Women and Domestic Ideology in Victorian Culture*. Ithaca, NY: Cornell University Press.
Nicoletti, L.J. 2004. "Downward Mobility: Victorian Women, Suicide, and London's "Bridge of Sighs." *Literary London: Interdisciplinary Studies in the Representation of London* 2 (1): n. p. Accessed Apr 17, 2017. http://www.literarylondon.org/london-journal/march2004/nicoletti.html.
———. 2007. "Morbid Topographies: Placing Suicide in Victorian London." In *A Mighty Mass of Brick and Stone: Victorian and Edwardian Representations of London*, ed. Lawrence Phillips, 7–34. Amsterdam: Rodopi.
Roberts, Andrew Michael. 1992. "The Gaze and the Dummy: Sexual Politics in Conrad's *The Arrow of Gold*." *Joseph Conrad: Critical Assessments*, ed. Keith Carabine, 528–550. Mountfield, East Sussex: Helm.
Wiley, Paul. 1966. *Conrad's Measure of Man*. New York: Gordian Press.

CHAPTER 6

The Adulteress and the Confines
of Marriage: "The Return" and *The Rescue*

*Lady—wife—mother! Should you ever be tempted to abandon your home, so
will you awake. Whatever trials may be the lot of your married life, though
they may magnify themselves to your crushed spirit as beyond the nature, the
endurance of woman to bear, resolve to bear them; fall down upon your knees,
and pray to be enabled to bear them—pray for patience—pray for strength to
resist the demon that would tempt you to escape.*
—Mrs. Henry Wood, *East Lynne* (1861, 116)

Conrad's debt to sensation fiction is particularly evident in "The Return"
(1898) and *The Rescue* (1920), both narratives that undermine the
Victorian idealization of matrimony and characterize the temptation
to escape from traditional marriage in adulterous liaisons. In particular, "The Return" reflects Mrs. Henry Wood's treatment of masochistic
servitude as requisite to proper marital submission of wife to husband,
and both "The Return" and *The Rescue* movingly depict the struggles of
women confined to marriages based on appearances rather than affection
or intimacy (Conrad 1924c, 1924d).[1] In Wood's *East Lynne* (1861), a
tremendously successful sensation novel that comes to define the genre,

---

[1]Perhaps unsurprisingly given the portrayals considered here, the composition of *The
Rescue* and "The Return" intersects. Conrad began writing *The Rescue* in 1896 (though
it was not published until 1920), Conrad began composing "The Return" in 1897 and
published it in *Tales of Unrest* in 1898. For more on this, see Knowles and Moore (2000).

© The Author(s) 2017
E.B. Harrington, *Conrad's Sensational Heroines*,
DOI 10.1007/978-3-319-63297-1_6

Wood famously calls on the reader— "Lady—wife—mother!"—pleading that she avoid temptation in the face of the "crushing" trials of married life (116).[2] Wood presents a self-destructive and self-denying vision of proper femininity as a remedy for the demon-haunted woman, in this case a married woman who is sexually unsatisfied. Since a woman who commits adultery prioritizes her own desires rather than subordinating them to the wants of her husband or the needs of the family, the adulterous woman can be read as a figure of rebellion; if depictions of the fallen woman typically center on the loss of idealized feminine purity, representations of the adulteress emphasize the failure to submit to the ideals of bourgeois family life.

In the mid-nineteenth century, novels and essays centered on the problem of "redundant" or unmarried women[3] typically characterize marriage as the inevitable personal and social remedy for the ills represented by the single woman; however, sensation novels centered on adultery and bigamy unsettle the certitude that marriage must be the solution to these social troubles represented by the *femme sole*. Wood's novel, one of the three sensation novels of the early 1860s that help define the form,[4] is centeredon anxieties about Victorian bourgeois respectability that are linked to women's sexuality and the dangers of women's illicit behavior to the family. In *East Lynne*, given the constraints of Isabel Vane's life and her lack of autonomy after her father's death, which lead to a marriage of convenience for her, Isabel's infidelity comes to seem understandable, even relatable, hence the warning to the reader. Wood frankly depicts Isabel's dissatisfaction in her marriage, but places the pleasure of Isabel's affair in the past, as Isabel repents her rebellion repeatedly in a masochistic series of trials that culminate in her

---

[2]The plot of *East Lynne* puts its heroine through a series of tormenting roles (her last, improbably, as the disguised governess for her own children in the household of her abandoned husband and his new wife) to atone for her scandalous audacity in leaving her kind husband and her children to be with a less worthy man who is more sexually attractive to her.

[3]In "Why Are Women Redundant?" (originally published in 1862), William Greg (1999) defines redundant women as unmarried women, the abundance of whom indicates "an unwholesome social state" (158). This category does not include domestic servants, since "they are fully and usefully employed" (161).

[4]As noted, along with *East Lynne*, Collins's *The Woman in White* (1860) and Braddon's *Lady Audley's Secret* (1862) establish the popular form of the sensation novel.

serving in disguise as the governess to the children she had abandoned and witnessing the harmonious family life fostered by her husband's new wife. As Marlene Tromp (2011) notes, "The affection readers felt (and continue to feel) for the fallen Isabel, however, seemed to undermine the tidy condemnation of her crime" in the novel (259). Wood idealizes the cuckolded husband in *East Lynne* as a model of bourgeois propriety, one of the self-made men who have become a kind of new gentry set in opposition to the rakish aristocratic villain who seduces and spurns a married woman. Thus, Wood associates bourgeois accession and respectability with personal and sexual satisfaction, as the abandoned husband forms a new marriage with a woman who properly shares his values and desires him.

As such, *East Lynne* unexpectedly provides a meaningful frame for "The Return," which sardonically critiques Victorian marital ideals by revealing a woman's dissatisfaction with her typical bourgeois husband, and for *The Rescue*, which elaborates on the ways in which the demands of conventional wifehood tax women's individuality and stint their development. As I noted previously, Conrad appears to have read Wood's novels both in his shipboard days and later in life (Jones 1999, 193), so the novel's admiring presentation of bourgeois life and anxieties over women's sexuality were likely familiar to Conrad and are familiar sensational themes. "The Return" considers women's sexual dissatisfaction and the dangers it poses to the family in the context of the New Woman at the turn of the century, likewise hinging on the ways in which wifely discontent and women's liberation threaten the bourgeois family, even as it exposes such family values as corrupt and self-serving. Conrad's depiction of Alvan Hervey in "The Return" mercilessly critiques the idealized vision of bourgeois domesticity—fostered by male dominance and womanly submission—that is depicted as a lost idyll in *East Lynne*, a space of formerly contented domesticity sacrificed to adulterous sexual desire. Likewise, Conrad depicts Martin Travers of *The Rescue* as a man whose existence is consumed by concerns about superficial respectability and a persistent anxiety that other men appreciate his importance. Travers's marriage stifles his wife, who can only uphold it by treating the "pageant" of their life skeptically and ultimately submitting to her husband's authority despite fully comprehending his weaknesses (*Res* 410, 412).

As in *East Lynne*, "The Return" and *The Rescue* portray traditional marriage as a sadistic bargain that requires a wife to be like the Herveys' sculpture, an image to which the story refers repeatedly, "the woman of marble, composed and blind on the high pedestal" that "seemed to ward off the devouring night with a cluster of lights" (182).[5] An image of woman as abstract ideal that echoes "personifications of Liberty and Justice," the statue functions ineffectually, unable to hold off the darkness, a beautiful bourgeois artifact meant to signify the Herveys' culture that actually exposes it as an illusion (Schneider 2003, 9). Treating Hervey's comfortable privilege with steady irony, Conrad exposes his blindness as a man averse to intimacy and self-knowledge and intoxicated by his own mastery, fostering a household in which "noble sentiments are cultivated in sufficient profusion to conceal the pitiless materialism of thoughts and aspirations" (121). Travers resembles Hervey in his bourgeois sentiments and pleasure in easy domination, and *The Return* echoes the figure of the Herveys' sculpture in its representation of Edith Travers's risky approach to the Malay settlement carrying a lighted torch that blinds her in the darkness; protected by her femininity and shielded by her veil, Edith glimpses a society where women rule as men do, but she can do nothing more than return to her pitiable husband to shore up his ego and resume her wifely role. Despite notable differences in style and subject, "The Return" is of a piece with other stories that critique bourgeois ideals in this same period before the turn of the century, such as *Heart of Darkness* (1899),[6] and it anticipates the cynical views on bourgeois manhood and the Victorian marital bargain that later appear in *The Secret Agent*. *The Rescue* revisits these themes, evoking the romance to consider in part the ways women are excluded from the subject role in the adventure story and left holding the torch as it were. Heliéna Krenn's (2000) commentary on the feminist context of "The Return" illuminates both works: the story "centers on the psychology of a man whose claim on the woman of his choice is challenged by a male rival and the woman's awakening consciousness of her self-worth" (5). Both "The Return" and *The Rescue* consider the ways in which women's self-worth is circumscribed by men's claims on women, and both stories examine the psychological hardship on men as they are confronted with the newly

---

[5]This is clearly an earlier iteration of Kurtz's painting in *Heart of Darkness* "representing a woman, draped and blindfolded, carrying a lighted torch" (Conrad 1924b, 79). Lissa Schneider explores the critical history and resonances of the images in her chapter "Iconography and the Feminine Ideal" in *Conrad's Narratives of Difference* (2003).

[6]Peter Keating (1985) and Lissa Schneider (2003), among others, note similarities in the themes and gender depictions in these two works.

conspicuous subjectivity of a formerly submissive wife. Each narrative offers the possibility of liberation or escape, yet, in the end, each wife makes the decision to return.

I

'Pon my soul, I did not know you could forget yourself to that extent.

—Hervey in "The Return" (*TU* 168)

As mentioned above, Conrad was not proud of "The Return," disparaging it in correspondence and in his Author's Note to *Tales of Unrest* (1924d). Since Albert Guerard's memorable dismissal of it in his 1958 *Conrad the Novelist* ("Conrad's worst story of any length, and one of the worst ever written by a great novelist," 96), many critics have comfortably set the tale aside—along with its Jamesian pretensions. Yet Conrad's experimentation as he depicts Hervey's inner life in "The Return" allows him to portray the effects of women's liberation on male identity, demonstrating the toll that male dominance and bourgeois ideology take on men as well as women.[7] The themes of "The Return" resonate with the earnest and deadly marital dynamics of "The Idiots" and *The Secret Agent*, as well as that novel's critique of the bourgeois elevation of sacrosanct ideals over human connections,[8] wryly disrupting Hervey's easy presumption that he possesses his wife as though she is a household accouterment. Telling the story largely, though not exclusively, through the indirect perspective of Hervey, a husband comfortably ensconced in unexamined bourgeois values and insulated by wealth, Conrad invites criticism of the kind of traditional masculinity that is structured by gender domination and unquestioned dominion at home and abroad. Almost a caricature with a "smouldering cigar between his teeth,"[9] Hervey moves through London "with careless serenity, with

---

[7] Keating (1985) reads "The Return" as a kind of rewriting of Ibsen's *A Doll's House* because of its similar themes and events.

[8] Gaetano D'Elia (1984) argues that, "Alvan Hervey is really the predecessor of the wordy zealots we will meet in *The Secret Agent* nine years later. Hervey's private lucubrations, crammed with religious excitement, will be transformed into the political arguments of the pseudo-revolutionaries in *The Secret Agent*" (38).

[9] The reader might connect Hervey as a triumphant, cigar-smoking commercial man in this passage from "The Return" with Heyst early in *Victory* (Conrad 2016), as he contemplates the ruin of the Tropical Belt Coal Company:

the tranquil ease of someone successful and disdainful, very sure of him-self—a man with lots of money and friends" (118, 119). Set against his solidity and self-confidence, Hervey's wife's revolt is timid and abortive, yet it unavoidably exposes the façade of their marriage, a hollow marital bar-gain, to Hervey, who realizes that his wife is incomprehensible to him.

Conrad begins the story with a damning depiction of a "band of brothers"[10] utterly incapable of the kind of idealized shipboard solidar-ity that readers find elsewhere in Conrad:

> Between the bare walls of a sordid staircase men clambered rapidly; their backs appeared alike—almost as if they had been wearing a uniform; their indifferent faces were varied but somehow suggested kinship, like the faces of a band of brothers who through prudence, dignity, disgust, or foresight would resolutely ignore each other; their eyes [...] had all the same stare, concentrated and empty, satisfied and unthinking. (118–19)

In this "sordid" urban environment, the men are like depersonal-ized automatons as they avert their eyes from even the most superficial human connection with likeminded men, unified in their ratified disre-gard for each other. This image offers the reader a terrifying vision of the "kinship" of male privilege in the blank stare, "concentrated and empty, satisfied and unthinking," of the City men who just exited the "inner circle train" (118). Elsewhere, Conrad will remind us of the privi-leged, dismal pattern of a life inhabited by such men who conform to an agreed-upon set of standards in the street and at home. Unlike Kurtz, these men do not need to go to the Congo to get the money to marry,

---

His nearest neighbour—I am speaking now of things showing some sort of anima-tion—was an indolent volcano which smoked faintly all day with its head just above the northern horizon, and at night levelled at him, from amongst the clear stars, a dull red glow, expanding and collapsing spasmodically like the end of a gigantic cigar puffed at intermittently in the dark. Axel Heyst was also a smoker; and when he lounged out on his veranda with his cheroot, the last thing before going to bed, he made in the night the same sort of glow and of the same size as that other one so many miles away. (20)

[10] Conrad's ironic invocation of the idealized comradeship "band of brothers" from the St. Crispin's Day speech in *Henry V* underscores his criticism of these men's unearned mas-tery in "The Return." The aged anarchist Karl Yundt in *The Secret Agent* also dreams of a" band of men absolute in their resolve to discard all scruples in the choice of means" (Conrad 1924e, 42).

but their lives are structured by a similar disjuncture between appearance and reality, and they also are capable of brutality.

We are meant to think Hervey is a good catch in the turn-of-the-century world of the story, "tall, well set-up, good-looking, and healthy," and he presumably possesses the ruthlessness of a good competitor in the economic marketplace, fulfilling the Victorian ideal of the good provider to his domestic angel (119). Conrad sketches Hervey in still greater detail: "his clear pale face had under its commonplace refinement that slight tinge of overbearing brutality which is given by the possession of only partially difficult accomplishments; by excelling in games, or in the art of making money; by the easy mastery over animals and over needy men" (119). This description of Hervey stands as a definition of a certain kind of British masculinity that Conrad is assessing here, men in the inner circle who recognize each other and whose masculinity is underscored by violence and the "easy mastery" it confers. Such men avoid testing themselves with truly difficult tasks, preferring instead the gratifying pleasure of dominance attained without too much effort or risk. Conrad references a series of roles conferred by privilege: sport, finance, and pure mastery; and he portrays these figures in domestic politics and colonial life as a satirical indictment of the economic men who buttress British patriarchy at the beginning of the twentieth century.

Opening the story with the succinct description of Hervey's preference for power conferred without difficulty foreshadows the story's ending: Hervey, incapable of getting to know his wife as an individual or of recreating the pretense of bourgeois marriage after his wife's scathing honesty, simply flees, underscoring his weakness and his cowardice. While the structure of the story alludes to the Victorian trope of the dishonored woman abandoned after a fall from grace, Conrad's descriptions and characterization undercut the husband's moral high ground, so that he is the dinosaur incapable of admitting the truth of his marriage or acknowledging his preference for mastery over his wife rather than intimacy with her. Such intimacy would require a desire for introspection on his own part, an uncomfortable self-knowledge that Conrad shows to be largely impossible for Hervey. As Celia Kingsbury (2000) remarks, "Hervey's superficiality is what we are to see and fear, to shudder at." Like his returned wife does initially, Hervey clings to the socially acceptable forms, the consensus of his class of men who find fulfillment only in conformity.

Conrad famously wrote to Edward Garnett that he wrote "The Return" "to give out the gospel of the beastly bourgeois" (Garnett 1928, 111), a remark which might explain in part the story's relentless probing, at times almost unbearable for the reader as well as Mrs. Hervey, of the tortuous rationalizations of Hervey's thoughts as he responds under stress: moving from violence to dejection, from shame to mastery. Conrad characterizes their marriage as a bargain between "cautious conspirators in a profitable plot": "They skimmed over the surface of life hand in hand, in a pure and frosty atmosphere—like two skillful skaters cutting figures on thick ice for the admiration of the beholders, and disdainfully ignoring the hidden stream" (123). While the critique of the Victorian marital bargain in which men and women negotiate for "profit" of various kinds is familiar in Conrad's oeuvre, this familiar image of domestic happiness—a couple skating in a winter idyll—cleverly becomes the reflection of the hypocrisy of this cold couple who refuse to look below the surface, the false image of harmony performed for onlookers. In her reading of the story, Deidre David (1976) comments, "This crucial passage suggests two central concerns of 'The Return,' self-conscious performance and the concealing and repressive mechanisms of middle-class culture" (138). The Herveys have hitherto assumed that the appearance of domestic bliss in accordance with the expectations of their inner circle of prosperous bourgeois patrons of the arts would substitute for the real thing.

When Hervey receives the letter his wife left for him, he is both "sick" and "humiliated," and the narration shows him grasping for how he "ought to" feel (127–128). Conrad portrays Hervey as disconnected from his own feelings, partially from shock but partially from the sheer superficiality of his reactions as he worries about how the situation will look to others. What kind of narrative should Hervey construct about his situation to save face? He feels so unmanned by his wife's departure that he wonders if he can preserve more dignity in his social set by pretending he had been beating his wife (132). Even her death would have been preferable—"And no one would have cared. If she had only died!"—since it would not have disrupted his sense of mastery in the same way (129). The narrative returns again and again to the "marble woman, decently covered" set amidst the Herveys' gallery of expensive treasures.[11] Ted Billy describes Conrad's critique of Hervey's appropriation of his wife as a signifier of his status: "Conrad heaps his scorn on the protagonist's naive belief that his wife is as dependable and predictable as a piece of statuary, a prized possession that he can count among his social assets" (179).

As a commodity, Mrs. Hervey (she is unnamed in the story) meets her husband's expectations, "The girl was wealthy, tall, fair, and in his opinion was well connected, well educated, and intelligent," but it is her restlessness that makes her vulnerable to the kind of marital bargain that Alvan Hervey represents: "She was also intensely bored with her home where, as if packed in a tight box, her individuality—of which she was very conscious—had no play. She [...] had not a thought of her own in her head" (120). The term "individuality" is repeated patronizingly to describe her, a term which both signifies her value as an artistic commodity (as such valued by her husband, a bourgeois patron of the arts, who has "artistic tastes—at home,"123) and situates her in the contemporary discourse on women's liberation. Yet her individuality is primarily expressed through "all manner of philanthropic work" and "various rescuing and reforming societies patronized or presided over by ladies of title" (121). Thus, Mrs. Hervey's individuality and artistic impulses serve to elevate the bourgeois Herveys, bringing them into a more elite social set defined by "ladies of title." Individualism here is merely another fashionable bourgeois attribute, until it inspires Mrs. Hervey to leave.

Her marriage is based on proper Victorian submission under the guise of sentiment: "Under the cover of that sacred and poetical fiction he desired her masterfully, for various reasons; but principally for the satisfaction of having his own way" (120). Here Conrad demonstrates the way in which representations of the idealized wifely role functions to oppress women (echoing the similarly sacred—yet hollow—ideals critiqued in

---

[11] In *A Wilderness of Words* (1997), Ted Billy reads this image as a reference to Robert Browning's "My Last Duchess," since Hervey, like the Duke of the poem, seeks mastery over a subordinate wife whom he sees as a kind of art object gracing his home (179). Also a man of "artistic tastes," Hervey fantasizes about his wife's death and resents that she seems to lack appreciation for the stature he has conferred upon her (*TU* 123). Browning's poem may be read as a scathing critique of hypocritical Victorian values, as the dominant husband, having ordered her murder, reduces his child-bride to a veiled portrait that gratifies him and serves as a warning to the man negotiating his next marriage. In "The Return," Conrad uses the image of the lifeless gallery of artistic treasures to convey the similar emptiness of this home, evoking the sterile dominance of another such husband.

Heart of Darkness), as he shows Mr. Hervey's pleasure in the "master-ful" role of husband. Mrs. Hervey's position emerges as a difficult one, since her sexual liberation as envisioned in the story can only be a choice between two men, and it is perhaps unsurprising that she returns to choose security and commitment over a new life or a tryst with the poet-editor of her husband's society paper.[12] Though the narration describes both of them as incapable of intimacy, Ruth Nadelhaft (1991) notes that this seems to wear more on Hervey's wife: "Though the narrative regularly describes Hervey and his wife as sharing equally in the mindless existence which skims over the surface of life, the imagery here suggests that the wife suffers from her imprisonment and from the airlessness of her life" (*TU* 122; Nadelhaft 1991, 70). Her honesty disrupts the pretense of their marriage, shattering Hervey's sense of his own mastery: "You are deceiv-ing yourself. You never loved me. You wanted a wife—some woman—any woman that would think, speak, and behave in a certain way—in a way you approved. You loved yourself" (177). These assertions mark the truth of the individuality that the narration earlier mocked as pretense, as she shows the kind of self-awareness that Hervey has studiously avoided; she insists on making the bargain between them explicit, telling Hervey that, had she believed in his love, she would have never returned.

David notes "Hervey's self-enclosed narcissism" when his wife returns: "He is described as a priest-like guardian of 'formulas, of rites,' exulted as he chants a stream of moral platitudes, and the assumption of his new role may be seen as defense against what is most threatening in his wife's behavior, a 'sinful self-forgetfulness' which he is afraid will be conta-gious" (David 1976, 141; *TU* 156). Hervey's wife's insistence on hon-esty, her awareness of their particular relationship throws Hervey because it refutes the notion that they are a generic wealthy bourgeois couple whose relationship is valuable primarily because it is much the same as everyone else's. Intimacy would require that Hervey acknowledge that he cannot fully conform to or take refuge in his class in the way he has assumed, which in his eyes is "self-forgetfulness" or forgetting one's place. In Hervey's eyes, his wife's individualistic actions are indecent: she "has become unknown to Hervey, an unquantifiable individual of her own mysterious volition" (Nadelhaft 1991, 75). The narrator defines her

---

[12]A separation also might have been economically risky for her, as William Bonney (1996) notes, "for the Married Women's Property Act of 1870 had done little to alleviate the financial vulnerability of women after marriage."

frustration: "That feminine penetration—so clever and so tainted by the eternal instinct of self-defense, so ready to see an obvious evil in everything it cannot understand—filled her with bitter resentment against both the men who could offer to the spiritual and tragic strife of her feelings nothing but the coarseness of materialism" (176). In his portrayal of her lack of understanding and Hervey's doomed attempt to address her deep feelings with "coarse" materialism, Conrad shows the hopelessness of their well-varnished union. Both characters fall into familiar gender types throughout the story, and they lack the ability to traverse the gulf in their understanding and expectations of each other.

She flees when he goes to embrace her in a fleeting moment of realization, which she misreads as sexual interest on his part. Presaging the marital dynamics of *The Secret Agent*, she turns to face him "swift and crouching" as though she is ready to fight or at least defend herself, the term "crouching" evoking an instinctual response that foreshadows the brutality that Hervey will threaten (178). Living on a street in which even the trees stand "in respectable captivity behind iron railings," the Herveys have repressed their genuine feelings, accepting a kind of respectable captivity (123), but as William Bonney (1996) wryly comments, "Hervey's wife can only temporarily be reduced to collaborative statuary." She desperately tries to assert a more genuine kind of individualism: "Alvan... I won't bear this." She began to pant suddenly, "I've a right—a right to—to myself..." (185). This statement recalls Susan Bacadou's plea in "The Idiots," as Conrad poses for the reader the extent to which women must live for others, that familially exacted tribute to Victorian patriarchy. In this may be the explanation for her return. If what she wants is autonomy, then leaving her husband for another man might offer only more of the same, so returning is better than exchanging one unenviable relationship for another.

If Mrs. Hervey has a right to herself, then Hervey's claim of possession can no longer be exacted; it is not perhaps surprising that he then "lifted one arm, and appeared so menacing that she stopped in a fright and shrank back a little," contemplating the violence that would allow him to dominate (185). This is the potential for a husband's brutality that has been implied since the beginning of the story, Hervey's pleasure in "easy mastery." She becomes fearful and questions the motivations for her own return: "He looked menacing. She thought of violence, of danger—and, just for an instant, she doubted whether there were splendors enough on earth to pay the price of such a brutal experience" (185). The earthly splendor of the Hervey's home makes a poor return indeed for the sacrifice of Mrs. Hervey's independence, as he repays her for her earlier rejection of him with "menace" and threat.

Initially, as he faces the effects of his wife's departure, Hervey desires to preserve the pretenses of the life he had: "the ideal must—must be preserved—for others at least," like Marlow tearing the scrawled postscript from Kurtz's report for the Society for the Suppression of Savage Customs after his death in *Heart of Darkness*[13] (*TU* 165). His wife's infidelity has taken away Hervey's sense of his own power, so that he is "like a prisoner in chains" before her, humiliated by "the thrust, insidious and penetrating" of her departure, which reads as a kind of sexual violence against him (133).[14] Gradually, he comes to consider the flawed basis for his marriage and his choices in life, but instead of coming to any understanding, he tries "desperately to relate what he has seen to his wife, to reduce his vision so that its cause may be attributed to his wife and her action. This way lies survival" (Birdseye 1977, 174). Lewis Birdseye captures Hervey's experience of a potentially disrupting realization about himself that he can only keep at bay by recalling himself to the subject of his wife's behavior, as he uses outrage at her betrayal to avoid the powerful experience of his own isolation. It would seem that Hervey's own departure at the end of the story should be based on some kind of realization about himself, but Conrad undercuts the possibility of Hervey's growth with as he falls into his familiar habits of mind: "His moments of perception of a truth beyond the conventional are hard-won, and so transitory that even as they are reached, they are re-obscured by Hervey's conventionality and egoistic anxieties" (Kramer 1988, 8). Hervey cannot do more than flee his newly honest wife's acknowledgement of her own dissatisfaction and their mutual isolation. She has admitted that she would not have returned had she believed Hervey loved her; in her eyes, the charade of their marriage is based on an implicit exchange that based more on affectation than affection. Their understanding—this marital bargain—is possible, at base, because of the dearth of emotion in their marriage.

---

[13] John G. Peters (2012) notes of Marlow in *Heart of Darkness*: "he finds it necessary to keep women in a separate sphere in order to maintain a place of refuge for men from the outside world" (97). While Hervey does not display Marlow's capacity for introspection, Conrad seems to be conveying a similar, though less elaborated, sentiment here.

[14] This might recall for the reader Winnie's thrust as she stabs Verloc before leaving him in *The Secret Agent* (Conrad 1924c).

Keating (1985) argues that, at the end of "The Return," Hervey's wife remains "weak" and that Hervey now has moral justification for his dominance rather than merely dominating his wife by his physical strength (229). But Hervey leaves in part because she stands up to him. She does not leave again, despite his "menacing" rhetoric and behavior, averring that she can "stand it" (185). In a sense, she wins the contest of wills at the end of the story, and Hervey cedes ground, never to return again. If she is shocked at his departure (the slamming door ironically echoing Nora's final departure in *A Doll's House*, as Keating notes), waiting "with parted lips and irresolute eyes," the reader can only appreciate being relieved of "the appalling clamour of his thoughts" (186, 185). It is difficult to imagine that she is better off with him.

Mrs. Hervey's victory has been her truth telling. Marlow chooses to tell the Intended a consoling lie that more deeply implicates him in the colonial corruption to which he might have borne witness in *Heart of Darkness*,[15] but Mrs. Hervey frankly acknowledges the truth of her marriage to her husband. If she does not choose to leave him, it is perhaps because she is less committed to her characteristic, performed "individuality" than she had believed—or simply because she realizes that fleeing her conventional husband for a somewhat less conventional lover will not significantly improve her subjugated position. Her familiar life of wealth and privilege might offer more security and material comforts in the long run than a hastily arranged liaison, but the reader also has no reason to assume that her lover is any more prepared than Hervey to appreciate Mrs. Hervey's individuality as a person who is a woman. Considering the political context of this story, Krenn (2000) sees "The Return" as documenting the inability of patriarchal institutions to adjust to women's increasing social consciousness and demands for more autonomy: "Written in the last decade of the nineteenth century when the heretofore unchallenged male world felt threatened by a new climate of gender relations and New Woman writing, 'The Return' is an examination of the accepted ideal of masculinity faced with the feminist attempt to establish new subjectivities" (4). Conrad exposes the extent to which Hervey's ego as well as his class sensibilities and aspirations require him to dominate his wife and portrays his "beastly bourgeois" musings as well nigh

---

[15] Peters (2012) notes that, "In the end, Marlow protects the Intended's world by lying to her," but such an act means he cannot "relinquish" Kurtz with the truth. (107).

unbearable to the reader. However, as in so many of Conrad's other portrayals, we are left with Mrs. Hervey "irresolute" on the cusp of something new, a sympathetic figure in her dissatisfaction, but one whose future is not narratable in the frame of this story.

II

Recalling *East Lynne*'s demon-haunted woman, the plot of *The Rescue*, like "The Return," hinges in part on the problematic marriage of a self-important man to an unsatisfied woman who is sexually attracted to another man. Though the genesis of *The Rescue* slightly precedes "The Return" and the novel's early composition overlaps with "The Return," the two texts are markedly different in style and scope. Yet, like *East Lynne*, "The Return" and *The Rescue* tacitly acknowledge that the wives' discontent goes beyond their apparent sexual frustration to their limited options as women in contemporary society. Ruth Nadelhaft (1991) reads "'The Return as "[a]lmost a precursor to *The Rescue*," since it "examines the difficulties faced by a young woman of intelligence and drive limited to marriage as a means of expressing herself " (70). Like *East Lynne*'s Isabel Vane before them, Conrad's portrayals of Mrs. Hervey and Mrs. Travers expose the shortcomings of traditional marriage, considering how women's economic and social position is established through savvy marriage bargains: in *The Rescue*, "the nature and extent of Edith Travers's misfortune testify to the terrible constraints on a woman's opportunities for choice and development in a world which makes marriage the test of judgment and the only avenue for development" (Nadelhaft 1991, 128). Nadelhaft's terms here, "choice" and "development" emphasize the way that an autonomous identity is barred to those who can seek it only through wifely submission.

Early in the novel, the Travers's traveling companion, D'Alcacer, puzzles over Edith Travers's choice to marry Martin Travers, a choice that he assumes must have been spurred by ambition as he notes her "disenchantment" with her husband (124). Conrad frames the initial perspective on the Travers marriage from outside as the curious D'Alcacer ponders her demeanor toward Travers and tries to divine Edith's motive in marrying him. Deriding their marriage as a blunder, D'Alcacer decides "such a successful mistake would explain completely her scorn and also her acquiescence" (123). D'Alcacer himself looks down on Travers, whose depiction strikingly resembles Hervey's in "The Return."

Travers desires self-aggrandizement at all costs, and D'Alcacer puzzles over a being "whose life and thought, ignorant of human passion, were devoted to extracting the greatest possible amount of personal advantage from human institutions" (123). Because Travers views financial profit as the primary motive for human interactions, an assumption that may be justified in his marriage, he is unable to negotiate properly with Tom Lingard, the captain of *The Lightning* brig and Travers's rescuer, whose motives are utterly opaque to Travers. His expectations informed by these bourgeois sentiments, Travers fears extortion and to be bested financially by Lingard, which would be an assault on Travers's pocketbook and, hence, his manhood. Lingard knows he needs to rescue the yacht's European passengers out of racial solidarity and for political expedience in the long run, but he cares deeply about his commitment to restore Hassim and Immada to their position as rulers, which represents, as Susan Jones (1999) notes, a "chivalric quest" (187). Travers's bourgeois calculations run up against the romanticized notions of heroism that Lingard cherishes as owner of his own swift and, in its own way, elegant brig; the uncomprehending Travers assumes he has met a pirate, when he has met an idealist, who hopes to honorably pay a debt and serve as the white savior who restores the Wajo rulers to their rightful place of authority. Lingard's position as a working-class sailor who made good in the goldfields and bought his own handsome ship represents a particular threat to the cultivated Travers, who concertedly works to shore up class hierarchies as a bulwark against his impotence when his ship is stranded.

Travers's class condescension offends Lingard from their initial meeting, though Lingard is the only immediate hope for aid for the Travers's stranded yacht, and Travers's sense of entitlement and skeptical treatment of Lingard evokes in Lingard "the birth of an unreasoning hate" (121). Later, once their intimacy is established, Lingard tells Edith, "If he hadn't been your husband I would not have put up with his manners for an hour"[16] (306). Disregarding the peril of their situation, Travers explains to Edith that he detests Lingard because he does not fully recognize and appreciate Travers's own importance as a man of high status. Like Hervey, Travers seems more concerned with the appearance

---

[16]As Harry Sewlall (2008) notes that Travers "has already demonstrated that not only is he the exact opposite of what a gentleman should be, but also an irredeemable snob and a virulent racist" (155).

of respectability than the state of his wife's emotions or their intimacy
(271). Tom Lingard strides onto the *Hermit* yacht as an idealized masculine type, whose virility and self-possession contrast the impotent
Travers, who must wait for a rescue or for higher waters to reach their
stranded boat. D'Alcacer is immediately attracted to Lingard, foreshad-
owing Edith's attraction for him; D'Alcacer mentions his strong liking
for Lingard as a counterpoint to the *coup de foudre*, the sort of passion
that will inflame Edith. Immada, too, senses the nature of Lingard's
and Edith's mutual attraction in that first meeting as she begs the fascinated Lingard to look away from Edith and effectively break the spell.
Immada presciently fears that Lingard's passion for Edith will draw his
engagement away from Hassim and Immada's cause, subordinating their
cause to the sexual attraction he feels for Edith, and she later accuses the
uncomprehending Edith: "You put madness into his heart, O!" (218,
234).

Lingard's and Edith's intimacy grows once Travers and D'Alcacer dis-
appear from their evening constitutional on a nearby sandbar, and she
is forced to rely on Lingard to protect her and recover the imprisoned
men. Edith's idealized European features and slim body crowned with
fair hair stir Lingard's desire, as the novel describes her as an exemplar of
her class who exists in a state of gentle, cynical rebellion against it. For
"King Tom" Lingard, she represents an unattainable European beauty
of higher class, and her interest in him is an affirmation of the influence
and high position he has been able to attain in these Malay waters. Her
husband will later accuse her of having taken pleasure in looking down
on the "best people" back in Europe, the ones he, presumably desires
to court: "Your conduct was, of course, above reproach; but you made
for yourself a detestable reputation of mental superiority, expressed ironically. You inspired mistrust in the best people. You were never popular"
(269). Recalling Hervey's anxiety over appearances, Travers clearly views
Edith's lack of popularity among the people in their set as a moral failing,
yet another failing of hers from which he must avert his eyes. She off-
handedly replies to her husband's attempt at a scathing criticism of her:
"I was bored" (269).

Travers believes his capture with D'Alcacer is an elaborate farce "[a]t
my expense," a deep conspiracy designed to defraud him, and he refuses
to acknowledge the danger in which he finds himself because doing so

diminishes his own importance (265–266). He does not want to admit that he is merely a pawn in local political intrigues, a way for an aspiring Malay like Daman to stake a claim on Lingard, who is much the more important man in this setting. To Travers, Edith's going inland with Lingard represents violating the respectability of their yacht and the white men on board whose duty it was to protect her (267). In fact, Edith's traveling with Lingard increases their intimacy, and Travers refuses to admire Edith's impulse as a wifely duty as he comments in a "slightly pompous" manner:

> No. As a matter of fact, as a matter of experience, I can't credit you with the possession of feelings appropriate to your origin, social position, and the ideas of the class to which you belong. It was the heaviest disappointment of my life. I had made up my mind not to mention it as long as I lived. This, however, seems an occasion which you have provoked yourself. It isn't at all a solemn occasion. I don't look upon it as solemn at all. It's very disagreeable and humiliating. But it has presented itself. You have never taken a serious interest in the activities of my life which of course are its distinction and its value. And why you should be carried away suddenly by a feeling toward the mere man [meaning Travers himself] I don't understand. (267–268)

Travers cannot credit Edith's coming as an understandable wifely choice to be inland where he is being held captive, instead choosing to view it as another proof of her immodesty and lack of respectability. Ironically, she is taking the risk of her husband's death quite seriously, as he attempts to reframe his mortal risk as Daman's prisoner as a drawing-room kerfuffle. Like Duke in Robert Browning's "My Last Duchess," Travers feels he has made a bad marital bargain in which his wife fails to stand in adequate reverence to his name; thus, Edith lowers herself in her husband's estimation by failing to seclude herself in the yacht as a domestic space. Travers feels the pressure of keeping up appearances even in this remote island setting where there are only three other European men to judge him. Edith tries to rally her husband, recasting her behavior as natural in a married couple. She asserts that her coming to him stands up to outside scrutiny, effectively arguing that her staying on the yacht would have been unconventional and perhaps cold: "My feeling was of the most conventional nature, exactly as if the whole world were looking on. After all, we are husband and wife. It's eminently fitting that I should be concerned about your fate" (268). The very nature of this exchange, as the couple argues about what behavior would have looked the most conventional on Edith's part, demonstrates the strain in their relationship.

Edith's rationalization does little to mollify Travers, and he once again impugns her character in a way that seems to cast her as Lingard's counterpart and inappropriately assertive and masculine: "It's my belief, Edith, that if you had been a man you would have led a most irregular life. You would have been a frank adventurer. I mean morally. It has been a great grief to me. You have a scorn in you for the serious side of life, for the ideas and the ambitions of the social sphere to which you belong" (268). Conrad here leaves the reader wistful for what might have been; Edith does have an adventure and betray her insufferable husband, but she does so only to return to him and presumably reassume her life of ennui. Edith cannot be a "frank adventurer" cut loose from the society's mores as even her infidelity is framed as a lapse that takes place within a frame of strict marital expectations. It seems a shame that her husband cannot respond except with disappointment to the very qualities that engage the reader: "All of the personal characteristics which make Edith Travers attractive to the reader and the outsider, D'Alcacer or Tom Lingard, are the qualities which offend and disgust her husband, to whom she is irrevocably tied" (Nadelhaft 1991, 128). When Travers accuses Edith of being "primitive" and "imperfectly disciplined," she gives the reader a glimpse of the depths of the dissatisfaction she has repressed, commenting that her "discipline has stopped at nothing short of killing" herself (270). Recalling the carefully veneered world of the Hervey household in "The Return," the narrator of *The Rescue* notes: "It was as if the polished and solemn crust of hard proprieties had cracked slightly, here and there, under the strain" (272). This "cracking" of surfaces is particularly evident when Edith assumes local dress.

When Edith travels inland with Lingard, she exchanges her European dress, damp yachting wear that is markedly inappropriate for the situation as she moves among Muslim men, for the splendid local clothes that Lingard has purchased in anticipation of Immada's restoration to rule. As Lingard works to secure the release of Travers and D'Alcacer, Travers objects strongly to seeing Edith move about publicly in such clothing, deeply concerned about what the clothing signals about her respectability (265). (He should, perhaps, be concerned about her growing intimacy with Lingard, but Travers seems determined not to look below the surface, transferring his qualms into formal objections about her wardrobe.) Edith acknowledges the propriety of her clothing in a realm that her husband refuses to recognize—"fit for a princess [...] of the quality, material and style custom prescribes for the highest in the land, a far-distant land where I am informed women rule as much as the men" (274). This jab at her husband shows her dissatisfaction with the subordinate wifely role, a role that particularly chafes given her superiority to him intellectually and in terms of her perceptions of others. For a moment, Edith offers the reader a glimpse of this "far-distant land" where women rule "as much as the men," a vision of equality that passes her husband by as he frets about her "native" dress.[17] She reminds her husband that she wears these clothes to be respectable in this situation—to travel safely and modestly among the Muslim men with whom Lingard will negotiate for the European men's release. Edith's use of Immada's clothes, effectively desecrates them since a reigning Immada would never wear clothes that another woman had worn, establishing the pull that each woman has on Lingard as he attempts to serve both their causes. The incongruity of a European woman in such garb also offends the old Captain Jörgenson, who is assisting Lingard. Jörgenson feels the local dress emphasizes her immodesty compared to Malay women: "To Jörgenson Mrs. Travers in her un-European dress had always been displeasing, almost monstrous. Her stature, her gestures, her general carriage struck his eye as absurdly incongruous with a Malay costume, too ample, too free, too bold—offensive" (363). If Edith feels her Malay dress might associate her with a society in which women might rule, Jörgenson sees this as an appropriation of local mores that amounts to a "monstrous" and bold assertion of self.[18] As it did for Lena in *Victory*, Edith's adoption of local dress signifies a profound departure from European proprieties that seems to be associated with her claiming possession of her own body and desires.

---

[17] Of course, Britain's Queen Victoria, who would have been the British monarch at the time the novel was set, did not rule "as much as the men," nor did her position as queen materially help women to better themselves politically or in domestic life. Edith seems to envision a world where she might don the appropriate clothes and assume leadership, rather than the hereditary ties of the monarchy in Britain (*TU* 274).

[18] While Robert Hampson views Edith Travers's dress as a "masquerade," Sewlall argues that her willingness to don these garments can be read as respectful: "For a woman coming from a conservative environment as she does, her decision to accept the habiliments of another race and culture, not to mention a religion that represents the traditional Other of her own, Christianity, is not to be taken lightly" (Hampson 2000, 180; Sewlall 2008, 123).

Earlier in her adventure, Edith admonishes Lingard, "And pray don't look upon me as a conventional 'weak woman' person, the delicate lady of your own conception," continuing, "Make that effort please against that conception of what a woman like me should be. I am perhaps as strong as you are, Captain Lingard'" (254). Edith seems to be trying to redefine herself in this new context, asking for respect and a kind of equality. As a European woman, she has been restricted in her pleasures, her freedom of movement, and her behavior, conscious of "living in front of a show" (303–305). When the time comes for Edith to act her part in the drama, she emerges bravely, using her very femininity as a shield to get to Lingard: "She was alone bearing up a blazing torch on an earth that was a dumb shadow shifting under her feet" (393). Again, Conrad uses the trope of the woman as light-bearer, the personification of cultural ideals, and Lingard is overwhelmed with desire at her self-possession and beauty.

As he pulls her into the enclosure, the narrative obliquely consummates their passion: "He didn't release his hold of her; his helpful and irresistible grip had changed into a close clasp, a crushing embrace, the violent taking possession by an embodied force that had broken loose and was not controlled any longer" (394–395).[19] The description concludes portentiously, "The inevitable had come to pass" (395). When a young man brings her the head scarf she lost as Lingard pulled her into the stockade, she uses it to veil herself even though she is going to see the European men, her husband and D'Alcacer: "This thing works both ways, as a matter of propriety or as a matter of precaution," since she fears that her face will betray her newly consummated passion for Lingard (399). Now veiled, she asks him, "Tell me, Captain Lingard, how many eyes were looking at us a little while ago?" but she then admits she does not care, since those beings are not of her world (400). Clearly, Edith's disregard for non-European eyes as witnesses to their embrace indicates the Eurocentrism that structures the Traverses' relations with the Malay population, but it also represents a powerful contrast to her husband's constant worry about proprieties. Fearing Jörgenson's judgment, Edith decides not to give Lingard the ring she carried, a message to Lingard that is mysterious to her, a

---

[19] See Joyce Wexler's (2018) excellent discussion of this passage and the novel in "Conrad's Erotic Women."

decision that helps doom Hassim and Immada, who have been taken captive. As Katherine Baxter (2010) comments, Edith has long been skeptical of European culture, but she has viewed Malay culture with a "romantic vision": "Whilst Edith explains that her sceptical vision is something that has affected her since childhood, it is clear that ethnic difference, perceived through language and appearance, reinforce her inability to grant the reality of the world in which she finds herself. Like Jim [in Conrad's *Lord Jim*], Edith's failure in this respect has devastating consequences" (126). Edith's failure to credit the ring and other aspects of the Malay plot as more than "romantic props" proves fatal for Hassim and Immada, who have also trusted Lingard as their rescuer (Baxter 2010, 126). Thus, Edith insists that Lingard value her and the Europeans over his commitment to Hassim and Immada, reinforcing her view of European centrality and solidarity, a presumption that Conrad critiques here.

Through D'Alcacer, Conrad makes the status of Tom Lingard and Edith Travers as iconic figures of romance clear, dramatizing their rapport and supplanting the Malay romance with the European one to tragic effect. As Gary Geddes (1974) asserts, "Conrad goes to considerable length in *The Rescue* to establish the image of Lingard as a figure from a simpler, more heroic age, or, rather, as a hero with values that are nobler than those of the petty, artificial world of the *Hermit*" (111). D'Alcacer muses that Edith serves as the kind of figure who inspires, "a representative woman," a description that both idealizes her and shows the confines of her position (411). Such women "decorate our life for us," but when they "leave the pageant they get lost" (412). D'Alcacer's reductive description of Edith as decorative and representative, a beautiful object in a world of male subjects, recalls aspects of both *Heart of Darkness* and *The Arrow of Gold* (Conrad 1924a, b). The image of Edith as the torch-bearer evokes Kurtz's enigmatic painting of such a subject and Marlow's assertion that women are "out of touch" and must be kept away from the real business of colonialism, which does not bear scrutiny (*HD* 59). Edith must suppress her skeptical viewpoint and rejoin the "pageant," which is necessary to the preservation of traditional society and its hierarchies. But Rita of *The Arrow of Gold* ultimately rejects her status as a beautiful *objet d'art*, disappearing from the pageant of European society that D'Alcacer cites, to free herself from the expectations of even the most well-meaning men. Edith, having played her role as a moral "adventurer" with Lingard and the Malays, in the disparaging words of her husband, will return to the pageant that is European life; however, "her disaffiliation from the moral structures of the mother country will problematise her return" (Jones 1999, 188). Edith's recent adventures might make it all the more difficult to resume her conventional life.

Having pondered the possibility of a society where women rule—or at least have more autonomy—she will become again a "decorative" wife, embracing the circumscribed role that she has been able to exceed in some ways on this adventure. Conrad demonstrates the parity between Lingard's class positioning and Edith's gender positioning in that, like Lingard, Edith must be diminished in European society. He can only be the consequential "King Tom" at a distance from such social mores, and she must reaffirm her marital compact as the lovely wife of a consequential man. Returned to his yacht, Travers finds the familiar surroundings "had soothed his vanity and had revived his sense of his own importance," but Edith suspects her husband is childishly exaggerating the after-effects of his fever to avoid confronting her (455). Before meeting Lingard, Edith dreams of him as a knight "vaguely recalling a Crusader," and Lingard does behave nobly, taking the blame for the abandonment of Hassim and Immada on himself as he tells Edith: "if you had given me the ring it would have been just the same" (458, 465). Lingard, devastated by his own betrayal of the Wajo rulers,[20] can only set course opposite to the Herveys' yacht, since no idealized union of Lingard and Edith Travers is possible.

Thus, like Mrs. Hervey, Edith makes her own return, clear-eyed about the compromise she is making in going back to her husband. Jones notes that Edith's realization of the "emptiness of her former life" provides one of the cruxes of the novel: "As the omniscient narrator enters Mrs Travers's center of consciousness, Conrad this time gives the woman the encounter with the 'heart of darkness'" (191). Unlike the Intended, Edith sees behind the veil, and understands both her husband's value and her own corruption. Edith casts her last meeting with Lingard partly in economic terms, asking both her husband and D'Alcacer whether they agree that "the uttermost farthing should always be paid," since she feels she owes it to Lingard for rescuing her husband and D'Alcacer—and for betraying his trust in not giving him the ring (456, 460). However,

---

[20]Robert Caserio (1985) notes how Lingard "is shown to diminish in stature as he becomes increasingly the guardian of the white ego and Western conventions" (128–129).

it is also clear to the reader how much returning with her husband will cost Edith. D'Alcacer predicts to Lingard that women like Edith who "leave the pageant" and presumably peer outside their constricted roles "end by hating their very selves, and they die in disillusion and despair" (412). D'Alcacer's vision represents a world where women must remain blind, bearing the torch, or else risk the profound dissatisfaction that comes with self-awareness. Robert Caserio (1985) reads Mrs. Travers as effectively a suicide like Jörgenson, "even though Mrs. Travers continues to 'live'" (147). Conrad envisages no place for a liberated woman in European society, unless perhaps in a fantasy romance with the impossibly attractive Tom Lingard. Both Mrs. Travers and Mrs. Hervey must return to their husbands, though Mrs. Hervey's honesty has cost her the farce of her marriage.

When Travers accuses his wife of a lack of decorum and "wilful bad taste," Conrad seems to be addressing the reader of popular genre novels as well: "You have always liked extreme opinions, exotic costumes, lawless characters, romantic personalities" (270). Presumably, Edith has used these trappings of romance to distract herself from the "monstrous" tedium, the utter boredom of her proper life. In Conrad's fiction, that "demon that would tempt you to escape," in Mrs. Wood's parlance, goes beyond unsatisfied desire to the issues of women's autonomy and subjectivity. Traditional marriage in "The Return" and *The Rescue* is informed by men's sadism and women's masochism, as wives have to annihilate their individuality and self-worth repeatedly to partake in a "pageant" inflected with implicit violence and menace toward rebellious women. In Conrad's treatment of the anxieties surrounding women's liberation and changing social mores, he depicts women's lives and the injustice they face as well as the difficulty of achieving real liberation for women. It is not surprising that Conrad uses such exotic tropes that self-consciously evoke popular fiction to dramatize Edith Travers's realization of her own confinement. Once her husband is kidnapped, Edith can assume the fantastic dress of a woman who rules and live the fantasy of a passionate reciprocal love affair. But, of course, such a vision of autonomous femininity can be nothing more than an illusion in contemporary British society, and Edith must return to act her part in the pageant with her husband. In "The Return" and *The Rescue*, such bitter returns to domestic life after infidelity represent the toll of a wifely rebellion that cannot be sustained as the "uttermost farthing" must be paid (*Res* 460). In these stories, Conrad uses the figure of the adulteress to expose the hollowness of the marital bargain and the pervasiveness of the patriarchal structures that support it, leaving Edith to forget herself in "that story" of an operatic passion that was "[m]ore real than anything in life" (301).

REFERENCES

Baxter, Katherine Isobel. 2010. *Joseph Conrad and the Swan Song of Romance*. Aldershot: Ashgate.

Billy, Ted. 1997. *A Wilderness of Words: Closure and Disclosure in Conrad's Short Fiction*. Lubbock: Texas Tech University Press.

Birdseye, Lewis E. 1977. "The Curse of Consciousness: A Study of Conrad's 'The Return.'". *Conradiana* 9: 171–178.

Bonney, William. 1996. "Contextualizing and Comprehending Joseph Conrad's 'The Return'". *Studies in Short Fiction* 33 (1): 77–90.

Braddon, Mary Elizabeth. 1862. *Lady Audley's Secret*. Leipzig: Bernard Tauchnitz.

Caserio, Robert. 1985. *Conrad Revisited: Essays for the Eighties*, ed. Ross C. Murfin, 125–149. Birmingham: University of Alabama Press.

Collins, Wilkie. 1860. *The Woman in White*. London: Sampson Low, Son, and Co.

Conrad, Joseph. 1924a. *The Arrow of Gold: A Story between Two Notes*. New York: Doubleday, Page, and Company.

———. 1924b. "Heart of Darkness". In *Youth and Two Other Stories*. New York: Doubleday, Page, and Company.

———. 1924c. *The Rescue: A Romance of the Shallows*. Garden City: Doubleday, Page, and Company.

———. 1924d. "The Return." In *Tales of Unrest*, 118–186. Garden City: Doubleday, Page, and Company.

———. 1924e. *The Secret Agent: A Simple Tale*. Garden City, NY: Doubleday, Page, and Company.

———. 2016. In *Victory: An Island Tale*, ed. J.H. Stape and Alexandre Fachard. Cambridge: Cambridge University Press.

David, Deidre. 1976. "Selfhood and Language in 'The Return' and 'Falk'". *Conradiana* 8: 137–147.

D'Elia, Gaetano. 1984. "'The Return' and Conrad's Umbrella". *The Polish Review* 29 (3): 35–41.

Garnett, Edward. (ed.). 1928. *Letters from Joseph Conrad 1895–1924*. Indianapolis: Bobbs-Merrill.

Geddes, Gary. 1974. "*The* Rescue: Conrad and the Rhetoric of Diplomacy". *Mosaic* 7 (3): 107–125.

Greg, William Rathbone. (1999) 1862. "Why Are Woman Redundant?". In *Victorian Prose*, ed. Rosemary J. Mundhenk and LuAnn McCracken Fletcher, 157–163. NY: Columbia University Press.

Guerard, Albert J. 1958. *Conrad the Novelist*. Cambridge: Harvard University Press.

Hampson, Robert. 2000. *Cross-Cultural Encounters in Joseph Conrad's Malay Fiction*. London: Palgrave.

Jones, Susan. 1999. *Conrad and Women*. Oxford: Oxford University Press.

Keating, Peter. 1985. Conrad's *Doll's House*. In *Papers on Language and Literature Presented to Alver Ellegård and Erik Frykman*, ed. Sven Bäckman and Goran Kjellmer. University of Gothenburg.

Kingsbury, Celia M. 2000. "'The novelty of real feelings': Restraint and Duty in Conrad's 'The Return'". *Conradiana* 32 (1): 31–40.

Knowles, Owen, and Gene M. Moore. 2000. "'The Return'". In *Oxford Reader's Companion to Conrad*, ed. Owen Knowles, and Gene M. Moore, 306–311. Oxford: Oxford University Press.

Kramer, Dale. 1988. "Conrad's Experiments with Language and Narrative in 'The Return'". *Studies in Short Fiction* 25: 1–12.

Krenn, Heliéna. 2000. "Conrad's Women and Art: 'The Return' and 'The Planter of Malata' as Signposts in Conrad's Creative Landscape". *Fu Jen Studies* 33: 1–15.

Nadelhaft, Ruth. 1991. *Joseph Conrad*. Atlantic Highlands, NJ: Humanities Press International.

Peters, John G. 2012. "Joseph Conrad's Heart of Darkness and the World of Western Women". *Studies in Short Fiction* 37 (1): 87–112.

Sewlall, Harry. 2008. "Liminal Spaces in Lord Jim and The Rescue,". *Conradiana* 40 (2): 109–128.

Schneider, Lissa. 2003. *Conrad's Narratives of Difference: Not Exactly Tales for Boys*. New York: Routledge.

Tromp, Marlene. 2011. "Mrs. Henry Wood, East Lynne." In *A Companion to Sensation Fiction*, ed. Pamela K. Gilbert, 257–268. Malden, MA: Wiley-Blackwell.

Wexler, Joyce. 2018. "Conrad's Erotic Women." *College Literature* 45. Forthcoming.

Wood, Mrs. Henry (Ellen). 1861. *East Lynne*. Leipzig: Bernhard Tauchnitz.

CHAPTER 7

The Embowered Woman as Enchanting Commodity: "A Smile of Fortune" and *The Rover*

Like the Lady of Shalott weaving her "charmed web," portrayals of the embowered woman abound in Victorian poetry and art, perhaps most famously in Tennyson's poems "Mariana" and "The Lady of Shalott" and in the respective paintings by John Everett Millais and John Waterhouse they inspired. By definition, a bower is a tranquil space, bounded by nature, where the cultivated individual might retreat from the pressures of urban life—or where a woman, like the Lady, might be sequestered from the world: "The little isle is all inrail'd/With a rose-fence" (1833, lines 28–29). The idyllic trope of the bower as blissful natural retreat can be set against representations of the bower as a place of unwilling confinement, the place where certain women might live in seclusion, waiting. The appearance of a devoted man to relieve isolation—a life deferred—is the fulfillment of the fairy tales such stories evoke. Mariana's depression and mental distress at her abandonment by her lover increase over the duration of the poem as she regards the gradual dilapidation of her home, the "lonely moated grange" that is the analogue for her mental state.

Joseph Conrad's 1910 story "A Smile of Fortune" and his 1923 novel *The Rover* pose a similar scenario in which the familiar figure of the professional seaman, given to reflection and whose life has been lived mostly away from women, ponders a disturbing, developing attraction he has for a cloistered woman who is disempowered and degraded in the eyes of others (Conrad 1923, 1924d). In these stories, Conrad pointedly alludes to the familiar figure of the embowered women through men's

© The Author(s) 2017
E.B. Harrington, *Conrad's Sensational Heroines*,
DOI 10.1007/978-3-319-63297-1_7

eyes, making her confinement explicit by framing it through the familiar figure. Like Mariana, Conrad's embowered women exhibit signs of mental distress while trapped in otherwise placid settings—the resentful Alice barely containing her animal fury in a beautiful bounded garden and the scarred Arlette haunted by visions of hellish violence in a coastal farmhouse. In "A Smile of Fortune," the narrator enters "a magnificent garden": "a brilliantly colored solitude, drowsing in a warm, voluptuous silence. Where the long, still shadows fell across the beds, and in shady nooks, the massed colors of the flowers had an extraordinary magnificence of effect. I stood entranced" (42–43). Then, "I had not noticed the girl before" (43). It seems that the young captain has entered his Eden, a place of hidden sensual beauty in which the presence of an unexpected "girl" makes erotic possibility explicit. He is "entranced" even before he sees Alice, the sequestered inhabitant of this enchanted place, who is here protected by her father from society's judgments and from the wiles of dangerous men.

Both "A Smile of Fortune" and *The Rover* allude to the fairy tale motif of the heroic male rescuer, juxtaposing it with anxieties about isolated women's vulnerability to sexual conquest. In *The Rover*, Réal's self-conscious struggle with his attraction for the haunted Arlette simultaneously erases her identity and expresses the motif of chivalry to the idealized feminine: "'Body without mind! Body without mind!' he repeated with angry derision directed at himself. And all at once he thought: 'No, it isn't that. All in her is mystery, seduction, enchantment. And then—what do I care for her mind!'" (214). In "A Smile of Fortune," the captain cannot restrain his ambivalent attraction to the embowered Alice he sees as "snarling and superb and barely clad," that illegitimate daughter hidden away from disapproval in her father's garden (58). Both the captain of "A Smile of Fortune" and Réal of *The Rover* seem conscious of the way their desiring gaze objectifies these troubled young women, initially an enchantment of the body without mutual feeling on the part of Alice and Arlette. This consciousness registers in self-disgust on the part of the men, themselves isolated and distrustful of their own desires. Conrad treats the men's appraisals of Alice and Arlette cynically, highlighting their positions of privilege with regard to the isolated women and fostering a critique of the double standard for women. Dramatizing the disjunction between those "enchanting" illusory figures and the women they overlay allows Conrad to critique reductive codes of romance, even as he acknowledges their prevalence, and, perhaps, inevitability.

In "A Smile of Fortune," the captain comes to desire Alice, lured by Jacobus and charmed by his daughter, who has as much of the sullen degenerate as the fairy tale princess about her. The story deliberately invokes both contexts, memorably giving her an unrestrained and at times almost feral demeanor, which stimulates his longing to make a conquest of her. In Conrad's ambivalent telling, the captain who finds Alice's social isolation and her frank refusal of contemporary social mores seductive ceases to desire her once his desire is returned. The captain, who had been ready to assume the role of chivalrous hero to Alice to fulfill his own fantasy of masculinity, slinks away, giving up his command and sacrificing his burgeoning career in the process. Ensconced in the Escampobar farm, the traumatized Arlette of *The Rover*, faced with the memory the atrocities she has witnessed and committed, lives in mental illness and social isolation. In depicting Réal's struggles with the ethics of his desire for Arlette, since such desire has the potential to be predatory, *The Rover* offers a glimpse at a kind of self-awareness on the part of Réal that is notably lacking in her other suitors. *The Rover* and "A Smile of Fortune" offer rich nuance in Conrad's self-conscious consideration of the ways gendered representation and even revulsion shape the desires of Réal and of the young captain. Conspicuously situating these heroines as the object of men's valuations, Conrad considers the connection between the isolation and psychological trauma these women experience and their desirability to men. As Arlette confronts her past victimization, she is able to reclaim her identity in the narrative, and Conrad represents her rehabilitation from the psychological damage she suffers in the absence of the ideal of benevolent paternalism, allowing readers to glimpse something of her internal life as she recovers.

Addressing the alienation of these characters in terms of gender, Conrad evokes another familiar Victorian figure, as so many Victorian novels, particularly novels influenced by Gothic or sensational motifs treat the themes of hysteria, insanity, and mental disease in women; however, as we might expect, Conrad alludes to such fiction in a larger consideration of male perceptions of female and male roles. In *The Rover*, as he had in The *Arrow of Gold* (1924a), Conrad considers the ideal of feminine purity in relation to violence and eroticism, particularly evoking the trauma of his experience of World War I in his treatment of the aftermath of the

Reign of Terror in *The Rover*. Furthermore, in recalling such traumatized or hysterical figures from Victorian sensation fiction through the perspectives of the men that surround them, Conrad draws attention to the unstable and contradictory nature of such portrayals, inviting the reader to contemplate the injustice these woman experience without envisioning a liberating alternative to the familiar endings of marriage or isolation.

I

"A Smile of Fortune" begins by considering the captain's commercial interests, as he hopes for a good sugarcane crop and high freights, and his problematic relationship with his first mate, whom the captain must tolerate after "snatching him out of the jaws of death" (4). The comic treatment of the captain's annoyance with Mr. Burns—in which the two men's uneasy pairing is colored by Mr. Burns's near fatality and the debt it implies on both their parts—wryly anticipates the captain's interest in Alice, whose attractions also have commercial implications. Humorously alluding to his own heroism in nursing his officer and the inconvenience it has since caused him, the captain reveals confidence in his ability to play the hero, despite his anxieties about meeting his ship's owners' expectations. This follows on his musing about the views of the island itself and how it might play a part in his prospects: "And I wondered half-seriously whether it was a good omen, whether what would meet me in that island would be as luckily exceptional as this beautiful, dreamlike vision so very few seamen have been privileged to behold" (3). Like so many Conradian seamen before him, this captain seems dryly aware of his own susceptibility and youthful vanity.

Noting the captain's early complaint that "horrid thoughts of business interfered with my enjoyment" of the view of the island, Daphna Erdinast-Vulcan observes that the "incompatibility of enchantment and business is thus established at the very outset" (*TLS* 3–4; Erdinast-Vulcan 1999, 136). Resonant images evoke the simultaneous losses of his fellow captains, from the old captain's grief over the loss of his figurehead in the Bay of Bengal (which he perceives as prefiguring his own demise) to the young captain's loss of his sick baby, as the lack of wind kept the ship suspended just out of reach of assistance outside the port (10–11). Such information reaches the narrator through Alfred Jacobus, who manipulates the captain for commercial reasons to solicit his business as a supplier of ship's stores; notably, Jacobus, who has a reputation for a lack of "personal character," will also try to interest the captain in Jacobus's socially isolated and disparaged daughter, another instance of the incompatibility of business and personal interests and one which causes the cocky young captain a significant professional loss (14). If the captain will come to desire Jacobus's daughter, Jacobus himself has already been pursuing the captain aggressively; when Jacobus appears with a large bouquet from his garden, the captain recounts his "jocular" comment to Jacobus: "he made me feel as if I were a pretty girl, and he mustn't be surprised if I blushed" (22–23). Telling the story in retrospect, the captain highlights Jacobus's conflation of his commercial interests with the personal ones he will soon advance, perhaps alluding to the captain's flight as a kind of emasculation.

Conrad underlines the hypocrisy of the island society, setting the social death of Alice's father Alfred Jacobus for his sexual scandal against the social acceptance of and approbation for Alfred's brother Ernest, who can openly employ (and routinely physically abuse) his mulatto son. Initially, the captain is bewildered when the youth manning the door of Ernest Jacobus's business office is reluctant to announce his arrival on a matter of business: "He did it at last with an almost agonized reluctance which ceased to be mysterious to me when I heard him being sworn at menacingly with savage, suppressed growls, then audibly cuffed and finally kicked out without any concealment whatever; because he came back flying foremost through the door with a stifled shriek" (25–26). The captain longs to advise the youth to assault his employer in retaliation when the captain suddenly notes the "extraordinary resemblance of the two brothers" Alfred and Ernest evident in the youth's face (26, 28). This moment of delayed decoding[1] on the part of the captain sets up his adversarial relationship with island society. After the captain realizes the youth's employer and abuser must be his white father, Ernest Jacobus, the captain looks down on Ernest, the well-reputed importer, and favors "the wrong Jacobus," Alfred, who has been cast out of society for his shameful affair and mocked for his evident sexual submission (13).

Since the captain has not yet been subject to his own enchantment, he maintains some ironic distance from Alfred's situation: "The grotesque

---

[1] "Delayed decoding" is the term coined by Ian Watt's in *Conrad in the Nineteenth Century* (1979) that describes Conrad's depiction of the deferred understanding that might follow a character's initial observation. For example, Marlow later realizes that the "little sticks" hitting his boat in *Heart of Darkness* mean he is under attack (Conrad 1924c, 110).

image of a fat, pushing ship-chandler, enslaved by an unholy love spell, fascinated me; and I listened rather open-mouthed to the tale as old as the world, a tale which had been the subject of legend, of moral fables, of poems, but which so ludicrously failed to fit the personality. What a strange victim for the gods!" (36). The captain's earlier musings as he reached the island show that he thinks himself a better protagonist for such an "unholy love spell," one which caused a married professional man to throw off his old life for the all-encompassing and humiliating passion that such an affair implies.

The captain self-righteously believes himself to be an ethical figure in that he is willing to counter popular opinion and object to both Ernest Jacobus's abuse of his son and to the presumption that one kind of illegitimate child is more socially acceptable than another kind. He offers a self-conscious objection to such problematic patriarchal presumptions that hinge in part on expectations about female sexual behavior: a woman of color's extramarital sexual relationship with Ernest Jacobus— be it forced or consensual—and the subsequent birth of their child fall within accepted social mores. However, Alfred Jacobus's scandalous social and sexual submission to the circus rider, who at one point is reputed to have publicly lashed him with her riding whip, puts him at the behest of a sexually and socially problematic women: "Most extraordinary stories of moral degradation" ruined Alfred's reputation at home, and he brings the circus-rider's child to raise as his own, though his paternity is not established (36). The class transgression, together with Alfred Jacobus's willingness to shelter and nurture a child of his lover whom he might not have fathered, cause him to be cut off from society and treated with utter disdain. Alfred Jacobus raises Alice not as a servant, but as his daughter. This parallel highlights gender and race as comparable categories (both children are subject to the father) yet also emphasizes the hypocrisy of the island society: an overt extramarital relationship with a woman of color does not challenge social mores given the problematic significations attached to dark skin, but an adulterous relationship based in sexual submission to a lower-class white woman threatens the social hierarchy and the marital contract that buttresses it. When the young captain complains to his friend about the faulty logic in this comparison, pushing for equality, the friend replies: "You don't understand. To begin with, she's not a mulatto. And a scandal is a scandal. People should be given a chance to forget" (38). It is offensive that Alfred brings Alice up as his daughter rather than disowning her, which perpetuates the memory of his scandalous association with Alice's mother. However, Ernest's treating his mulatto son as an employee is no scandal at all, since an illicit relationship with a woman of color does not represent the same kind of transgression. It is "shocking to the respectable class" that Alfred treats Alice as his daughter rather than as a "scullion" (38). To the captain, this implicit comparison between the brothers makes the brother Alfred appear "a decent sort of fellow" by comparison (32).

When Alfred Jacobus initially appears on board the captain's ship, the captain mistakes him for Jacobus's brother to whom the captain has been referred and wonders presciently, "Was this white magic or merely some black trick of trade?" (7). Indeed, the captain's attraction to Alfred's daughter Alice seems at first to be fortuitous, but the captain will later dismiss it as a "trick of trade" on the father's part. The captain, however, seems to be wholly unaware of the extent to which Alice, as the subject of the parley between Jacobus and himself, has been abused, as they ironically fulfill her fears about the threat that men represent, culled from newspaper stories of marauding men in the streets of European cities. To her, the civilized world outside of her bower is full of threatening male violence.

The captain offers a surprisingly self-aware representation of the extent to which his desire objectifies, even disregards the woman in question. This Alice, ensconced in the walled garden of her father's home, is carefully isolated, removed from her father's world and her island town, which judge her so harshly for her father's sin against sexual respectability. Christopher GoGwilt (2011) notes the way the story is structured by "distorted allusions to fairytale, fable, and romance patterns," and these familiar motifs seem to be deliberately fractured and incomplete in "A Smile of Fortune" (Conrad 1923, 67). Conrad depicts a fantasy garden that feels miles away from the town (42). The narrator has been told to imagine Alice's mother as a "painted, haggard, desperate hag," which implies a disturbing vision of a potential future for Alice (37). The captain's initial description of Alice herself is full of atavistic details that contrast the European proprieties on which Alice's companion tries to insist: Her "black, lustrous locks twisted anyhow high on her head, with long, untidy wisps hanging down on each side of a clear, sallow face" (44). Alice seems unconscious of the duties of a young woman toward her father's invited guest and business partner: "She leaned forward, hugging herself with crossed legs; a dingy, amber-coloured, flounced wrapper of some thin stuff revealed the young supple body drawn together tensely in the deep low seat as if crouching for a spring. I detected a slight, quivering start or two, which looked uncommonly like bounding away" (44). She looks like a "startled wild animal" to the captain, who also appreciates the "scantiness of her attire" by Victorian sartorial standards (44). Alice's unladylike and unfiltered reaction to the captain allows her to be frank about her distrust of him and dislike of the society he represents, as well as about her eventual desire for him. If she is brutish, it is arguably her atavism that exposes the respectably concealed subtext of men's mercenary erotic and commercial instincts in the story.

In an analysis of *Alice in Wonderland*, Nancy Armstrong (1999) notes that Carroll's Alice, whose body changes size with her appetite, represents a kind of threatening instability: "Like those of working-class and native women, [Alice's] body is potentially out of control and, by its very nature, in need of regulation" (221). Despite her father's genteel aspirations, Conrad's Alice also represents a body that is "potentially out of control," since she is scantily and inappropriately attired, she refuses to participate in social conventions and niceties, and her very existence recalls the explicit details of her father's sexual scandal. The captain's desire for Alice is generated in part by the extent to which her father's insistence on social niceties and a veneer of propriety fail to mask her rebellious nature or her sexuality.

Jacobus has ensconced his problematic daughter in a lovely garden, protecting her from the judgmental island society and hiring her a proper companion as if to elevate her status. Conrad evokes the fairy tale of the embowered princess sardonically, since the captain, despite his early delusions of his own heroic capacity, ultimately refuses to rescue the princess, even with significant commercial inducements from her father. Thus, the narrative dismantles the captain's fantasy of his chivalrous masculinity. Alice's behavior marks a direct rejection of the socially appropriate upbringing that her father wants to impose on her, yet the captain finds her pose a kind of "sombre seduction" (68). When the captain briefly embraces her, he notes, "the first kiss I planted on her closed lips was vicious enough to have been a bite" (69). Her behavior inspires in him a kind of brutalizing desire to possess and contain her, as though her degradation frees him from the expectations of civilized courtship (and ironically fulfilling her fears about men from London and Paris), evoking Armstrong's (1999) concept of the "degraded double of the ideal

English woman" whose role is to "[ensure] that the bond among family-minded men remains strong even when they are far away from home" (241). Indeed, the captain realizes that he cannot continue to pursue such a partner; once she returns his desire, he will realize "clearly with a sort of terror [his] complete detachment from that unfortunate creature" (79).

In *Conrad and Women*, Susan Jones (1999) considers the way Alice resembles the African woman of *Heart of Darkness* more than she does the Intended: Alice "subverts the role represented by the white woman of ['Heart of Darkness']—the Intended—by refusing to adopt the image of idealised European femininity. As the narrator watches Alice, she awakens in him a sense of doubt and lack of confidence in his identity" (183). Ensconced in her enchanted garden, Alice's refusal to participate in the expected rituals and exchanges with an eligible suitor sets her apart from the predictable traditions of European femininity. Her frank revulsion and animal resistance spur the captain's desire. Again and again in their visits, the captain's gaze, which depicts Alice as seductively atavistic, fixes on Alice's body in parts: her throat, her feet, her limbs, her hair. Such figurative dismemberment culminates in what seems like an invitation to or fantasy of violence in the story: "And it was her smooth, full, palpitating throat that lay exposed to my bewildered stare. Her eyes were nearly closed, with only a horrible white gleam under the lids as if she were dead" (*TLS* 66). Alice assumes this vulnerable pose only to break it, opening her eyes and tell the narrator that, if he were to imprison her, she could strangle herself with her own hair (66). Alluding to and rejecting the Rapunzel story of escape from captivity from the Brothers Grimm, Alice's striking hair would serve to frustrate as well as stimulate the desires Alice attributes to the captain, the intimate weapon for her suicide.[2] Readers might also associate this image with the Victorian poet Robert Browning's (1888) poem "Porphyria's Lover," a first-person dramatic monologue about a man who strangles his unfaithful lover with her hair, so he can more fully possess her. Certainly, the embowered Alice has been raised to fear men and the violence they can wreak.

---

[2] Daphna Erdinast-Vulcan (1999) considers the effects of Conrad's allusion to *The Tempest*: putting the young captain in "the role of the rescuer" and drawing on "the idiom of fairytales," Conrad might be seen as casting the young captain of "A Smile of Fortune" in a kind of "parodic inversion" of *The Tempest*, though the story ultimately offers a more ambiguous conclusion than such a description implies (139, 135).

To entice Alice, the captain has to prevail over her fears of male violence shaped by news accounts from London and Paris: "She had formed
for herself a notion of the civilized world as a scene of murders, abduc-
tions, stabbing affrays, and every sort of desperate violence" (60). Her
understanding assumes a racial character based on these accounts, since
the only crime of any consequence on the island is "only amongst the
imported coolie labourers on sugar estates or the negroes of the town"
(61). As her companion points out, stirring Alice's panic, white men
commit these horrific crimes from the European newspapers, and such
sailors who are the associates of her father would be the "lowest of the
low" in Europe (756). GoGwilt (2011) considers the ways in which the
narrator's struggle to alleviate Alice's fears or put them in perspective
diminishes her position, mocking the fears her companion is encouraging: "This dispute offers a particularly striking example of the way the
narrator constitutes a European self over against Alice's Creole lack
of a European self" (74). Alice's fears of being subject to a threatening masculinity are directly related to her father's manipulations: "It
is not for nothing that the girl's worst visions take the form of a business deal between her would-be suitor and her father" (Erdinast-Vulcan
1999, 138). Jacobus has considered the captain and seems to view him
as a good prospect for Alice, deliberately throwing them together as a
condition of doing business with him, hoping to establish a business
relationship by encouraging a personal one. Yet the captain's interest
immediately diminishes once he senses Alice's returned desire for him
when she answers his kiss, ironically fulfilling her fears about European
men.

Ultimately, the captain realizes he is incapable of flouting social expectations to the extent that a relationship with Alice Jacobus would entail;
his instinctual desire for her is mixed up with a kind of powerful disdain
for what she represents. In abandoning her, he is not so principled as
he imagines, and he is aligned with the forces of patriarchal control in
the island society that he so disdained; as Erdinast-Vulcan (1999) comments, "The bourgeois ethos which the narrator has formerly scorned
now becomes the standard on which he acts" (141). Though the narrator appears to despise the intolerant society that dominates the island, he
also recognizes the social liability of a liaison with Alice, and he gives up
his flourishing career to extricate himself from the business and personal
entanglements in which Jacobus has ensnared him, rejecting the kind of
ending signified by his rescue of Alice's lost slipper in the story.

His attraction for Alice relies on an imagined version of her—the embowered, disgraced woman, a liminal creature of eroticized degeneracy—rather than any real mutuality or understanding that they share, and the captain portrays his attraction as intoxicating, disgusting, and ultimately a "lost illusion" (78). Jones explains, "The price of his 'cruel self-knowledge' is to lose hope of ever knowing the object of his desire. The power of the onlooker, predicated on implied possession of the viewed object, is diminished, while the image of Alice herself attains a startling presence as she resists her attachment with palpable energy" (183). To the reader, who can only know Alice through the captain's account, Alice's position of energetic resistance is indeed striking. Isolated in her island garden, she resists her father's pressure to conform to gender norms and social convention, as well as his implicit understanding with the captain about her own availability as a commodity from him, the seller of ship's stores. The captain is fascinated by her resistance, which he reads as both feral and radical, counter to the hypocritical value system imposed by island society, the bourgeois value system to which he ultimately capitulates.

Like Tennyson, Conrad uses the image of the bower to disrupt the implicit fairy tale and its expectation of the chivalrous man fated to rescue the isolated woman and help her achieve a proper marriage. No traditional marriage resolution awaits Alice, whose desires have been awakened and who has become aware of her abandonment. Rather than a place of peaceful retreat, the bower is a lush, Edenic prison for a woman stunted by the assiduous care of her parental guardian, a woman whose knight turns out to be distinctly unchivalrous. The daughter of the circus rider is not a suitable marriage prospect for the captain, but a version of the circus sideshow exhibit, whose freakish—and sometimes rebellious—animality ultimately frightens the captain away. The bower itself becomes a formally enclosed space for Alice as a character, one from which the prospect of escape is a narrative impossibility, one that is suffocating in its dreary confinement.

II

Old faces glimmer'd thro' the doors
Old footsteps trod the upper floors,
Old voices called her from without.

—Alfred, Lord Tennyson, "Mariana"
(1845, lines 66–68)

Like Tennyson's Mariana, Arlette in *The Rover* is haunted by visions of the past, which sometimes engage her more than her present inter-actions. Mariana's abandonment by her lover leaves her desolate and depressed, and she longs for an absent man to come and relieve her isolation.[3] The poem dramatizes the extent to which women's lives are bound up in the promise of a union with a suitable man, and certainly the Victorians, who had many young men bound up in military service all over the globe, were used to this fairy tale promise being unfulfilled as it was for Alice in "A Smile of Fortune." Yet, unlike Conrad's Alice and Tennyson's Mariana, Arlette will achieve the fairy tale ending, a mutu-ally satisfying union with a man who understands the nature of her past trauma and desires her. Arlette's embowerment is connected as much to her mental state as to her habitation, the remote coastal farm where she grew up, and her formerly happy home comes to serve as a kind of clois-ter where she can grapple with her demons.

Arlette's experience of—and participation—in the killings of the Reign of Terror and the mental deterioration that results from it prob-lematize her femininity and isolate her from her housemates and neigh-bors.[4] Her degeneration proves an unwelcome reminder of the politics of revolution and its human cost. Figuratively, Arlette, whose scars of bru-tal damage are hidden behind a placid exterior, calls to mind the Rita's double, the "mutilated dummy" from *The Arrow of Gold* (1924a, 21). The portrayal of George in that novel makes Réal's self-awareness in *The Rover* notable, since he is aware of the way in which his desire objectifies Arlette and is troubled by it. Réal sees in her the double of his own tragic alienation, longing for more intimacy beyond his infatuation, yet Arlette continues to relive the horrific trauma of her lost youth.[5]

---

[3] Tennyson derives Mariana from the character in William Shakespeare's *Measure for Measure*. The poem takes place before her lover returns in the plot of the play and does not envision the possibility of any relief for her.

[4] Arlette's mental state might reflect the "shell shock" that traumatized soldiers in World War I, including Conrad's son Borys. See Hampson (2012, 156–59). Certainly, Conrad's displacement of the Great War onto the Terror reflects another kind of embowering, con-taining the more immediate horror of World War I in the horrifying violence of the past, a memory that cannot be fully contained.

[5] Arlette's experience in *The Rover* closely resembles the experience of Countess Stéphanie de Vandières in Honoré de Balzac's 1830 story "Adieu." The countess, still a young woman, was separated from her guardians, caught up in Napoleon's retreat after the invasion of Russia in 1812. She becomes "le jouet d'un tas de misérables," literally the toy or plaything of the wretched retreating soldiers, desolately following the army for two years, and goes mad (1001). Eventually, the countess's lover recreates the scene of their separation, and she recovers her senses for a moment, only to die in his arms.

Like Rita, Arlette of *The Rover* is beautiful, but her innocence and feminine purity are tainted by her experience of and her participation in the Reign of Terror, which have left her, as Réal exclaims, "Body without mind!" (Conrad 1924d, 214). When her Royalist parents come to claim her from her convent school in Toulon, they are caught up in the violence and die in front of her. A *sans-culotte*, Scevola recognizes her from home and saves her, hoping to possess her and her parents' farm. Caught up with Scevola's band, she avoids participating in the violence until, "I let myself go at last. I could resist no longer. I said to myself: 'If it is so then it must be right" (155). Arlette's trauma, bound with her own guilt, is something she is forced to relive constantly as Scevola returns home with her. Her aunt, who remained at the farm, prevails upon Scevola not to have sex with Arlette when he returns with her, maintaining that in her deranged state, she is unable to give consent, so he lurks about their dwelling, sexually as well as politically frustrated in the aftermath of the Revolution, waiting to take possession of Arlette.

When her Aunt Catherine first sees Arlette, she is "pale like a corpse out of a grave," and "helpless as a little child" (91), the very description evoking her lost innocence and her trauma at witnessing her parents' death, which have paradoxically, protectively returned her to her early childhood haunts and the care of her aunt. Catherine continues, "I undressed her and examined her all over. She had no hurt anywhere. I was sure of that—but of what more could I be sure? I couldn't make sense of the things she babbled at me" (91). Catherine here testifies to Arlette's apparent sexual purity—her body, at least, evidences no hurt or violation—while Arlette's babbling frightens Catherine with the horrifying possibility of "what more" Arlette might have seen or experienced. As such, the family farm serves as a sanctuary for Arlette, but it also traps her in a static environment as Scevola lies in wait. Recalling the dummy-as-double image of Rita, Arlette has been reduced to a child-like state by her experience of violence, yet she retains her allure for men: as J.H. Stape (2000) notes, "Mainly hinted at, Peyrol's sexual interest in Arlette is displaced into the distorting mirror of Scevola, whose neurotic and latently violent interest is an attempt to dominate the young woman" (321). As Scevola openly longs for Arlette, an intimate threat of lurking violence from the traumatic past, the lieutenant, Réal, distrusts his growing desire and affection for her, since he mistrusts her mental state. During the years that elapse in the narrative, Peyrol's interest in Arlette is shown to be more paternal than erotic; in returning to the land of his birth, he, too desires reconciliation with his past (Hampson 1992, 279–280).

Arlette's experience is framed by the aged, roving seaman Peyrol's return. He fled, stowing away on a boat as a small boy, after waking next to the dead body of his mother. He fled without knowing his name, forced to craft his identity and shift for himself with only the faint memory of his past. Peyrol arrives apparently satisfied with his checkered past, but he, too, needs to reconcile himself to his early life. Like Peyrol, Arlette has been orphaned and scarred by the loss of her familial security and her place in life, but her memories are laden with horror and guilt. The depiction of Arlette recalls women's limited autonomy and Flora's dispiriting position in *Chance* (Conrad 1924b). While Peyrol and even Réal sublimate their childhood trauma in demanding careers, Arlette can only haunt her parents' farm, surrounded by reminders of her loss and complicity.

When Peyrol first makes his way to the Escampobar farm, Michel harbors doubts about his patriotism because Peyrol's manner of shaving (with a looted English razor) recalls the priests Michel has known. In the disorienting aftermath of the Revolution, the performance of patriotic purity becomes essential to social intercourse and self-protection, though such demands gradually diminish as the novel progresses. Peyrol's patriotism has been questioned frequently, since he served at sea during the revolution, and he is perceived rightfully as more pragmatic than ethical in his shipboard life. Yet the gentle Michel's questioning, together with Arlette's query, "Are you a patriot?," demonstrate concisely the nature of life at the farm, which is full of suspicion and competing personal agendas (20). Even in this remote spot, the brutal politics of the Revolution have infused the atmosphere with distrust and the potential for violence, along with the scars of past violence. Michel describes the "master" of the farm, Scevola, as one of the "best" of the "drinkers of blood," the sort of revolutionary who gloried in violence as a sanguinary indulgence for which politics gave him an excuse (20).

Arlette, greeting Peyrol in the dated, distinctive Arlesian clothing of her mother, strikes an odd figure, holding a conversation with Peyrol as her eyes dart around the empty room "as though Peyrol had come in attended by a mob of shades" (21). While reaching for her recently deceased mother's clothing might have been a practical matter, it also indicates Arlette's desire to reach back to the past, to the sheltered upbringing represented by her mother's familiar, brightly colored clothing. When Arlette mentions having lived as a child at the farm, Peyrol, conscious of his own advanced age, replies with emotion, "You are but little more than that now" (21). In being a victim—and eventually a perpetrator—of such horrific violence, Arlette can call up some recollection of her early innocence only by costuming herself as a woman like her mother, yet such clothes must evoke simultaneously her own loss. When, in this first meeting, Arlette confidentially asks Peyrol, "Have you ever carried a woman's head on a pike?" the nature of her experiences becomes clear to him and to the reader (22). She must come to terms not only with her victimhood and powerlessness in the face of violence, but also with her own acts of violence and capacity for violence. As Michel notes, when there was "more of that work than the guillotine could do," "[t]hey had to kill traitors in the streets, in cellars, in their beds. The corpses of men and women were lying in heaps along the quays" (20). Even in her traumatized state, having participated in such opportunistic killing, bloodshed nominally justified by politics, Arlette cannot ignore her own guilt, her implication in inhuman crimes like seeking out victims in their beds. Arlette finally tells Peyrol, "You may stay. I think we shall be friends. I'll tell you about the Revolution" (23). When he objects, she firmly replies, "It must be so" (23). Indeed, the story of the Revolution has become the only narrative about herself that Arlette can tell, a story that she can only supersede by choosing to rejoin the world of the living, leaving her "shades" behind. It is no wonder that Peyrol shouts to Arlette's aunt for a bottle of wine upon Arlette's departure.

In the isolated world of the Escampobar farm, Arlette's youth and beauty signify her sexuality and desirability, especially in relation to the example of her aunt, who spent her desire in her youth on an unattainable priest, yet Arlette's disengagement from the world around her and emotional damage mark her as victim and perpetrator in ways that problematize her womanliness, setting her apart from the men on the farm. However, unlike Rita in *The Arrow of Gold*, Arlette's trauma and loss of purity are not associated with her sexuality: "In the figure of Arlette, Conrad clearly presents a figure who has been traumatized, not by early sexual experiences, but by her exposure to the sights and experiences of the battlefield" (Hampson 2012, 175).[6] The harrowing loss of innocence experienced by this sheltered, convent-educated young woman represents the kind of wartime trauma that is associated with both men and women, but her response to the trauma resembles more her aunt, who withdraws

---

[6] Thus, as Hampson (2012) notes, that Freudian "sexualized account of trauma has been replaced with the desexualized account that developed during the First World War" (175).

from society when she does not die from her love for the priest, than men like Peyrol and Réal who repress their early trauma to make their way in the world. Ultimately, they follow the path Mrs. Fyne points out when lamenting the "miserable dependence of girls" in Flora's case in *Chance*: "But a young man—any man—could have gone to break stones on the roads or something of that kind—or enlisted—" (Conrad 1924b, 172). These men embrace hard labor and ultimately enlist (though Peyrol deserts in his youth) to make their way in the world, when all Arlette can do is return to her parents' farm in their blood-laced tartane in the custody of the blood-thirsty and desiring Scevola, who seeks to benefit personally from the changes wrought by the Revolution.

"Pity may be a crime" attests Scevola in conversation with Peyrol, dissatisfied that "there has not been enough killing" (27). The novel implies that Scevola's bloodthirsty participation in the Revolution occluded his incapacity and petty nature; Arlette's aunt recalls that before the Revolution, "He was the butt of all the girls, mooning about amongst the people outside the church on feast days" (92). Now, frustrated by Arlette's sexual remoteness and knowing himself to be an object of scorn and derision in the town, he longs to return to killing as a means of establishing his position and demonstrating his manhood. The narrative implies that Scevola wants Arlette as the remedy to his emasculation (in the manner of the similarly aggressive and opportunistic Schomberg of *Victory*), though his parasitic desire for her will ultimately end in his death in Peyrol's plot to save Réal, a death that the lawless Peyrol believes to be utterly justified. The narrator remarks on Scevola's unsuitability to his present life: "the patriot dragged his dirty clogs low-spiritedly in the fresh light of the young morning, in a way no worked on the land would ever do at the end of a day of toil" (39). When Scevola went into town to confront the priest who returned to their local parish some time after the Revolution, he was forced to flee, while the locals taunted him with the cry, "A mort! A mort le buveur de sang!" (41). In the retelling, Peyrol comments dryly, "It takes some pluck to face a mob of angry women" (41). While Arlette's participation in the violence haunts her, for Scevola, this very participation vindicates his desire for her; of her youthful convent education he comments: "No lessons of base superstition could corrupt her soul"; "I brought home a patriot" (33). Scevola seems to view Arlette as a spoil of war, along with her family farm, and his malignant presence there makes him an outsider, even among the farm's motley crew of inhabitants. Yet Scevola's bald desire for Arlette despite her mental state also serves as a reflection of the other men's conflicted longing for her, as well as the ethical dilemma that her continual trauma invokes.

When Peyrol first encounters Arlette, her listlessness and disengagement strike him; she reacts even to the sound of shoes on the floor: "The clatter of the clogs made her raise her black, clear eyes that had been smitten on the very verge of womanhood by such sights of bloodshed and terror, as to leave in her a fear of looking steadily in any direction for long, lest she should see coming through the air some mutilated vision of the dead" (49). Indeed, the reader is invited to watch Arlette and the symptoms of neurosis she displays in something like a "medical observation" (Hampson 1996, 152). Conrad draws the connection to purity through the language of desire that emerges in the description of her case, her "clear eyes that had been smitten on the very verge of womanhood" not by passion (as one might expect, and in the manner of her aunt) but by violence. Though Arlette is not the only haunted character, the severity of her mental distress serves to mark the others' afflictions; the Escampobar farm becomes a kind of asylum for each individual that inhabits it, as Conrad sketches a series of orphaned, dislocated characters. As Hugh Epstein (2005) explains, "what afflicts all these characters" is "that their more intense life is lived elsewhere, in visions, memories, or obsessions, or is withheld from them, and self-expression is replaced by an intentness spent in watching others and in interpreting the hints of incomplete utterance" (105). This dislocation and the failings of these characters to communicate contribute to the feeling that each is just biding time in this place.

When Peyrol confronts Arlette about her nighttime roaming, she confesses that her heart drove her out at night, a more natural restlessness, yet the English officer covertly approaching the farm from the water is frightened by her ghostly appearance: "there glided without a sound before his irresolute eyes from somewhere a white vision—a woman. [...] 'I won't say she froze my blood, sir, but she made me cold all over for a minute.' [...] 'She looked crazy'" (49, 62). Conrad deliberately casts Arlette as a kind of uncanny revenant, a symbolic representation of the damage wrought by the machinations and plotting of the decidedly masculine world that surrounds her. The virginal convent girl lost her innocence in violence, and Conrad revives her through her sexuality. Her growing awareness of her own bodily desire forces her consciousness back to the present and to the pleasures of the body; this depiction ironically contrasts that of her Aunt Catherine, whose girlhood passion for the local priest caused her to isolate herself, giving up on the possibilities of her sexuality. Catherine's sexual dissatisfaction looms large in the text, an unrealizable desire that prevents and protects her from marriage.

Certainly, some part of Arlette's attraction for Réal has to do with the fact that he is her counterpart, "the son of a ci-devant couple—small provincial gentry—who had both lost their heads on the scaffold, within the same week" (70). He also suffered from the loss of his family, sublimating his grief into professional success in the navy by acquired by "sheer merit"; however, his past isolates him, making him deliberately "self-contained" and without friendships (70–71, 117). Old Peyrol is the first to have "broken through" the reserve of this "orphan of the Revolution," impressing him with his insight and knowledge of the sea (71). As Réal contemplates his as-yet-unexplained naval assignment at the farm, he thinks about Peyrol as having been "next thing to a pirate" at times in his past life, which causes Réal to treat him skeptically (71). When Réal asks Peyrol if he has experience of prison, he bristles, then speaks of two adventurous escapes from enslavement before schooling Réal on manhood: "But don't you talk to me of prisons. A proper man if given a chance to fight can always get himself killed. You understand me?" adding later "Naturally any death is better than a prison. Any death!" (73, 74). Réal's contemplated naval intrigue has him considering the likelihood of a stint in an English prison in service of France in the hope of misleading the enemy with false intelligence. The suffocatingly close atmosphere of the farm also evokes confinement and is likewise suffused with plotting and false intelligence.

The haunted feel of the household is finally broken when Arlette fixes her thoughts on the present and acts on her growing and seemingly reciprocated passion for Réal. She calls to her aunt, "I am awake now!" (146). Peyrol's friendship (and what the narrator describes as his "power to soothe her aimless unrest," 146) and Arlette's return of present feeling and desire gradually improve her mental state: she exults in "the enormous change implied in the fact that every day had a to-morrow now, and that all the people around her had ceased to be mere phantoms for her wandering glances to glide over without concern" (146). In coming to see the pleasurable possibility of a future with Réal after a decade of traumatized disengagement, Arlette recovers her sense of time, remarking on the promise of "all the days to come" (223). She banters with Peyrol, teasing him good-naturedly, "Say, you, Papa Peyrol—don't you like me anymore?" (174), and he replies wryly, "I don't know whether I didn't like you better when you were quieter" (174). The narrator remarks on her renewed youth in the presence of her graying elders, Peyrol and her aunt: "Vitality streamed out of her eyes, her lips, her whole person, enveloped her like a halo" (175). This physical vitality demonstrates her liberation from the trauma that has circumscribed her and her embrace of her passion and desire for Réal.

Throughout her secretive transformation, the narrative describes Réal's chivalrous struggle with his own desire: "Honor, decency, every principle forbade him to trifle with the feelings of a poor creature with her mind darkened by a very terrifying, atrocious and, as it were, guilty experience" (209). His physical passion for Arlette in the face of her mental infirmity shames him; he asks, "What has become of my rectitude, of my self-respect, of the firmness of my mind?" (210). It also recalls Scevola's violent passion for Arlette, which he subdues because of her aunt's ethical scruples about Arlette's mental state even as he waits, presuming his possession of her. The unsavory aspect of the contest for Arlette further challenges Réal's rectitude, and it is only through Arlette's direct acknowledgement of her passion for him in light of her renewed self-awareness that they can come to an understanding about their mutual feeling. Furthermore, Réal here resists his desire to objectify Arlette, to use an imagined version of her as the basis for his affection for her. The immature George of *The Arrow of Gold* (1924a) longs to keep Rita as an object of admiration, loving her at a distance that facilitates his fantastic vision of her, apparently reserving some part of this distance even when they flee to live together (Conrad 1924a). In *The Rover* (1924c), however, Réal rejects his own desire to appropriate her image and finds an answering passion.

The joint future of Arlette and Réal can only be assured when Peyrol sacrifices himself for them, taking on Réal's intentionally doomed military mission: Hugh Epstein (2005) observes, "Peyrol's longing for Arlette and his jealousy of Réal remain unarticulated but observable, tightening the psychological knot of what otherwise might have been only a service matter" (107). Peyrol's altruistic action recalls the notion of chivalry, in part reintroducing the genre of romance (with a kind of fairy tale formula that includes hidden treasure, as Katherine Isobel Baxter (2010) notes, 146), and yet, as Epstein asserts, "an aspect of the skeptical inheritance in this novel is that the salvation offered by Peyrol to Réal and Arlette is not divorced from an intense assertion of self" (107). Peyrol's sacrificial act is not self-effacing, but an assertion of patriotism and vitality in the face of his realization of his own aging and the passion of the young couple. The ending foregrounds Peyrol's heroism and his "large heart," as the surviving, contented inhabitants of the Escampobar farm ponder his character in his absence (286). In the novel's resolution, Arlette has gone on to a happy life with Réal, her violent past and lost years unremembered as her character disappears into her wifely role.

This disappearance bows to the convention of the kind of fairy tale—or Victorian marriage plot ending—that *The Rover* and "A Smile of Fortune" seem to be working to problematize or even dismantle, as Conrad critiques the commodification of women within the very kinds of plots that seem to demand men's complicity in their objectification. The captain of "A Smile of Fortune" admits defeat at Jacobus's hands, since he cannot continue in his business dealings in the area without accepting marriage with Alice as part of the deal. Alice is simply left to wait in her garden, her fears about European men ironically justified by the captain's behavior. He has overcome her reservations about men and about the nature of his desire for her, but he does so only to abandon her. The captain's enchantment becomes merely an embarrassing memory for him in light of his renewed submission to his bourgeois sentiments. In Conrad's sobering ending, no prince will rescue Alice, nor can she be negotiated on her father's market. She remains ensconced in her father's domain, and, in exposing the father's machinations and the captain's qualms, Conrad invites criticism of Alice's subjection. In *The Rover*, Arlette is positioned initially as a queer ghostly figure—the echo of Wilkie Collins's (1860) famous woman in white, who is also mentally impaired and fearful of violence—a figure whose identity is virtually erased by her trauma. Yet her positioning shifts dramatically as she reengages with the world, and her transformation, inspired by her passion for Réal, is her own doing. She is not seduced by Réal; instead, Arlette realizes her own desires and acts on them, assuming control of her life. Having recovered herself, Arlette rejects the blighting influence of Scevola for a more satisfying union, one that reclaims the family farm and sets right the legacy of violence after the deaths of Arlette's parents.

Yael Levin (2004) claims of Conrad's oeuvre, "Whether man, woman, or illusion, the Conradian object of desire is never fully 'there'" (127). "A Smile of Fortune" dramatizes how the captain's illusions about his own maverick sensibility as well as his erotic fantasies about rescuing the embowered woman cause him to objectify and disregard Alice. Like *The Arrow of Gold*, *The Rover* considers the ways a traumatized woman can be reduced to a prop for desire. On Conrad's part, such self-conscious portrayals of the way genres like the fairy tale or the romance eroticize the absence or weakness of heroines invite critical analysis of the very genres that Conrad uses to structure these novels (see Hampson 1996, 144). In the broader context of Conrad's late novels, such portrayals might be seen to go further, probing modernist ambivalence about changing gender roles by portraying the inadequacy of these generic representations and the absent women at the heart of them.

REFERENCES

Armstrong, Nancy. 1999. *Fiction in the Age of Photography: The Legacy of British Realism.* Cambridge, MA: Harvard University Press.

Balzac, Honoré de. (1830) 1979. "Adieu." *La Comédie Humaine X: Études Philosophiques*, 960–1014. Paris: Gallimard.

Baxter, Katherine Isobel. 2010. *Joseph Conrad and the Swan Song of Romance.* Aldershot: Ashgate.

Browning, Robert. 1888. "Porphyria's Lover." In *The Poetical Works of Robert Browning*, vol. 5, 191–193. London: Smith, Elder, & Co.

Collins, Wilkie. 1860. *The Woman in White.* London: Sampson Low, Son, & Co.

Conrad, Joseph. 1923. "A Smile of Fortune." In *Twixt Land and Sea*, 3–88. Garden City: Doubleday, Page and Company.

———. 1924a. *The Arrow of Gold: A Story between Two Notes.* New York: Doubleday, Page, and Company.

———. 1924b. *Chance: A Tale in Two Parts.* Garden City: Doubleday, Page, and Company.

———. 1924c. "Heart of Darkness." In *Youth and Two Other Stories.* New York: Doubleday, Page, and Company.

———. 1924d. *The Rover.* Garden City: Doubleday, Page, and Company.

Conrad, Joseph. 2016. *Victory: An Island Tale*, ed. J.H. Stape and Alexandre Fachard. Cambridge: Cambridge University Press.

Epstein, Hugh. 2005. "The Rover: A Post-Skeptical Novel." *Conradiana* 37 (1–2): 101–118.

Erdinast-Vulcan, Daphna. 1999. *The Strange Short Fiction of Joseph Conrad: Writing, Culture, and Subjectivity.* Oxford: Oxford University Press.

GoGwilt, Christopher. 2011. "Conrad's Creole Family Romance and 'A Smile of Fortune.'" *Conradiana* 43 (2–3): 67–79.

Hampson, Robert. 1992. *Joseph Conrad: Betrayal and Identity.* New York: St. Martin's Press.

———. 1996. "The Late Novels." In *The Cambridge Companion to Joseph Conrad*, ed. J.H. Stape, 140–159. Cambridge: Cambridge University Press.

———. 2012. *Conrad's Secrets*. Basingstoke, UK: Palgrave Macmillan.

Jones, Susan. 1999. *Conrad and Women*. Oxford: Oxford University Press.

Levin, Yael. 2004. "A Haunting Heroine: The Dictates of an 'Irrealizable Desire' in *The Arrow of Gold*." *The Conradian* 29 (1): 127–138.

Stape, J.H. 2000. "The Rover." In *Oxford Reader's Companion to Conrad*, ed. Owen Knowles and Gene M. Moore, 317–322. Oxford: Oxford University Press.

Tennyson, Alfred. 1845. "Mariana." In *Poems*, 10–14. London: Edward Moxon.

———. 1833. "The Lady of Shalott." In "'The Lady of Shalott' (1833 & 1842 Versions)." *The Camelot Project*. University of Rochester, http://d.lib.rochester.edu/camelot/text/tennyson-shalott-comparison.

Watt, Ian. 1979. *Conrad in the Nineteenth Century*. Berkeley: University of California Press.

CHAPTER 8

Conclusion: A Woman Alone

When Alfred Hitchcock loosely adapts Conrad's *The Secret Agent* as
Sabotage[1] in 1936, he makes a surprising deviation from his source,
offering the character of Winnie Verloc a happy ending, one that is seemingly a throwback to the kind of Victorian marriage plot resolutions that
Conrad so effectively dismantles in many of his novels and stories, perhaps a version of the upbeat Hollywood ending for movies that can be
both appreciated and reviled.[2] *Sabotage*, a product of Hitchcock's early
years directing films in Britain, makes many changes to the novel's plot
and characters to streamline it and make it comment more immediately on the political context in Britain and on the continent in the years
preceding the Second World War. In his chapter on *Sabotage* and *The
Secret Agent* in *Modernism, Media, and Propaganda*, Mark Wollaeger
(2006) persuasively argues that, in *Sabotage*, Hitchcock "aimed to rede-
ploy Conrad's novel, itself consumed with by the problem of persua-
sion, as propaganda for himself in order to earn a ticket into the greater

---

[1]The same year, Hitchcock also adapted Somerset Maugham's *Ashenden* with the title
Secret Agent, which meant that Conrad's title for the novel could not be used for the film.
Sabotage was released as *A Woman Alone* in the United States.

[2]While Conrad's novels *Chance* and *The Rover* end with a marriage or the prospect of
one, this is unusual in Conrad's oeuvre. Each frames the marriage with another loss.

© The Author(s) 2017
E.B. Harrington, *Conrad's Sensational Heroines*,
DOI 10.1007/978-3-319-63297-1_8

resources of the American studio system" (41). While the substitution of a happy ending for Conrad's dark and ironic one is perhaps understandable in the context of such a motivation, considering the film as an adaptation, this ending is problematic and, arguably, gratuitous—and, as such, highlights the very issues with women and representation that are at the heart of the present study. Rather than delve into the more disturbing personal and political motivations and implications of Mrs. Verloc's violence, Hitchcock simply attaches her to another man who is fascinated by her beauty and vulnerability. Several decades after Conrad wrote *The Secret Agent*, Hitchcock felt the need to reinstate a more conservative resolution for *Sabotage*.

Writing in 1948, W.H. Auden memorably describes the endlessly reproduced cultural fantasy encapsulated in those "stories of strong silent men and lovely girls who make love in a beautiful landscape and come into millions of dollars" (157). Although women's roles and opportunities have changed significantly for the better from the early twentieth century to the twenty-first, popular culture still continues to refrain the kinds of gendered melodrama and structural gender norms that Conrad so effectively critiques in his writing. If Lombroso's taxonomies of criminal types have lost credence in contemporary society, our culture remains suffused with reductive constructions of gender and representations of women whose attractiveness is contingent on sexual purity and submission. Réal's struggle in *The Rover* with the ethics of being attracted to a traumatized woman who cannot consent and Heyst's fear in *Victory* that his attraction to Lena allows her to manipulate him instinctively for her own ends, for instance, reveal anxieties about gender and power that recall familiar tropes in current popular culture. Even if the terminology has changed, we still read and watch stories about "strong silent men" and those "lovely girls," women who are tainted by their sexuality in ways that are not possible for men, women whose individuality and empowerment cast them as harsh and unfeminine, women for whom some version of the marriage plot is the ultimate, and perhaps only, logical ending. There remains a concerning topical relevance in Conrad's complex depictions of women's and men's struggles with confining expectations with regard to gender and power—and the alienation that results from them—depictions that focus more on the loss such expectations engender and avoid easy and palpably false narrative resolutions.

In *Sabotage*, Hitchcock changes the family business from the Verlocs' pornography shop in *The Secret Agent* to a cinema, an effective segue to another form of representation that is staged, eroticized, and broadly appealing.[3] While the pornography and anarchist publications in the Verlocs' shop are, as we have seen, dull and lackluster rather than transgressive, *Sabotage* allows Mrs. Verloc to be drawn into a screening of the Disney film *Who Killed Cock Robin?* just after she learns of Stevie's death, and she is reluctantly engaged by the film's lighthearted comedy [which, as Paula Marantz Cohen (1994) notes, reflects the cartoon-like scenes in *Sabotage* as Stevie makes his way across London, scenes that immediately precede Stevie's death (206–207)]. Mrs. Verloc's pleasure in the film's antics is cut short by Cock Robin's being shot by an arrow, a scene that causes the audience to erupt in laughter as it plunges her into horror, forcing her to recall Stevie's death. Like the audience for the seemingly harmless *Cock Robin* film, many viewers of popular films take pleasure in the fantasy of violence such films proffer. If pornography and anarchist rags are the more covert pleasures of the Verlocs' seedy Brett Street shop, the cinema offers the kind of communal pleasures that can engage a broad audience; movies offer the viewer the chance to experience and validate a series of popular representations in a social setting, like the particular pleasure of enjoying both the antics of Cock Robin and then his probable demise.

Sabotage's resolution supplies the audience with a reassuring ending that returns the lovely and delicate Mrs. Verloc[4] to the kind of male guardianship from which she has just violently released herself, though this time her suitor is on the right side of the law. The film was released as *A Woman Alone* in the United States, a title that emphasizes Mrs. Verloc's position as a victim, though, intriguingly, Mrs. Verloc is never actually alone except in her marriage; after an explosion destroys the evidence, Mrs. Verloc moves directly from murdering Verloc to the protective arms of the police detective who loves her. In drawing attention to her plight, the alternative title *A Woman Alone* also highlights the narrative possibility upon which the film has actually foreclosed, the possibility of an independent life, though Winnie's suicide in *The Secret Agent* forecloses on that as well. Paula Marantz Cohen (1994) notes the

---

[3]Among others, Wollaeger (2006) explains that in the early part of the twentieth century, cinemas generated "cultural anxiety" associated particularly with the "darkened cinemas" as "places of moral corruption" (44).

[4]The name Winnie is not used in the film, where the character is simply referred to as Mrs. Verloc. The actress Sylvia Sydney also presents a different physical type than the Winnie Verloc that Conrad describes.

implications of the repeated variations on the family dinner, which precede the stabbing at the final Verloc family dinner: "Far from discrediting
the original image of the family at the dinner table, the stabbing scene
serves to reinforce that image as a generic symbol. Patriarchal authority,
domestic security, the duty to care for children, and for children to obey
and trust in parents are all given support, even though the particular family in question has been betrayed on all these counts" (205). Arguably,
Hitchcock frames Verloc's betrayal more directly as the justification for
his murder, rather than as a broader critique of the traditional social
mores and male dominance that the film supports. Even a story informed
by the dark and disturbing gender critique of *The Secret Agent* can be
adapted as a crowd-pleaser in which a "lovely girl" suffers the outrage of
being married to an inappropriate man, the saboteur of the title; after surviving the tragic loss of her brother and acting out violently, she is able
to find the right kind of "strong silent man" and be better served by the
benevolent paternalism of her culture. If there is anything to undercut
this simple *précis* that I have just given, it is perhaps the traumatized look
that remains on Mrs. Verloc's face in the film even after the detective Ted
Spencer saves her, and perhaps our memory of Ossipon from Conrad's
novel, who immediately realizes the disadvantages of taking up with a
woman capable of stabbing her husband to death. Reading between the
lines, perhaps the happy marriage plot will not do in *Sabotage* either, and
Hitchcock identifies himself with the perpetrator of outrages that Conrad
finds in himself in the Author's Note to *The Secret Agent* (xv).[5] Wollaeger
(2006) describes "Hitchcock's superior ability to ironize the conventions

---

[5]Cohen (1994) notes that Hitchcock plays up an implied comparison between the
Professor in *Sabotage*, who triggers the bombing in the cinema that masks Mrs. Verloc's
crime, and Hitchcock himself as the filmmaker:

> Obviously intrigued by the metaphorical correspondences between the bomb expert
> and the filmmaker suggested by this metaphor [in the novel, the Professor can trigger
> a bomb on his body to deter the police that is made "on the principle of the pneu-
> matic instantaneous shutter for a camera lens" (*SA* 66)], Hitchcock changed the
> Professor from a lean and solitary monomaniac into a rotund, fumbling eccentric, pro-
> ducing his bombs within an amusingly disreputable family setting (in the movie, the
> Professor's "cover" is a bird shop in Islington, the site of the Gaumont-British studio
> where Hitchcock made the film). As if he needed to drive home the point, he cast in
> the role an actor who bore a striking resemblance to himself. (202)

of popular entertainment without emptying them of consolation" (69). If the viewer feels something of a *frisson* at Mrs. Verloc's rapid and perhaps ill-advised segue into a new relationship, such misgivings are undermined by the sympathetic portrayal of the heroine and the power of the marriage plot that Hitchcock has just deployed. The viewer cannot believe that Mrs. Verloc is capable of killing anyone but her politically problematic and amoral husband Verloc, the man responsible for Stevie's death, and it seems as though her union with Ted redresses a wrong, giving her security and generous, if possessive, affection—and perhaps the chance to bear children of her own. Even if we view Hitchcock's resolution as purely formal, the director turns away from Conrad's complex presentation and critique of patriarchal strictures on gender from the novel, depicting the plot largely as a problem that can be resolved rather than a darker meditation on the stakes of gender oppression for a young woman. Thus, the transgressive possibilities of Mrs. Verloc as a saboteur fail to be realized in the film in a meaningful way.

In contrast to Hitchcock, Conrad's power to provoke derives from a consistent refusal to capitulate to the familiar narratives and representations he evokes; his facility in depicting and subverting—even sabotaging—such representations of women as a means of commenting on contemporary society and how it conceives of women as individuals is striking. As we have seen, Conrad's self-conscious borrowings allow him to look forward as well as back, and they offer perspectives not just on women characters but on how such women, as well as men, understand themselves culturally. By depicting heroines who are violently frustrated and who cannot truly be mastered, Conrad evokes and builds on the familiar sensational woman. So often sensation novels ultimately repress the rage and frustration of the women they so memorably evoke, a move that Hitchcock mirrors in *Sabotage*, but Conrad uses such figures to explore the rebellion that has been repressed in their confining marriage plots and carefully constructed endings. Conrad's treatment of women is thus central to his depictions of men and masculinity, even as Conrad clearly portrays the particular social forces that shape women's lives, including the repression and the gendered violence to which they are frequently subject.

Though Conrad was hardly a proponent of the politics of women's liberation, his repeated, subtle, and attentive depictions of men's and women's circumscribed gender roles must be perceived as to some extent political, and they continue to resonate. By alluding to, borrowing, and

reassessing familiar representations of women, Conrad frequently highlights women's subjugation on the basis of gender, and his stories and
later novels show how much this subjugation costs women and men,
even the men who try not to perpetuate it. As Marianne DeKoven
(1999) explains, much of what drives the modernists' innovation in form
is their "irresolvable ambivalence towards powerful femininity" (174).
If women's liberation is impossible in Conrad's worlds, nonetheless, he
distinctly critiques the destructive effects of patriarchal structures on
women's identity and autonomy, and the way such structures further isolate men and women by substituting pretense for intimacy. In so doing,
Conrad uses Victorian generic representations in a distinctly modernist
way, effectively interrogating the ways in which women are hemmed in
by traditional cultural institutions and elaborating on the way in which
such institutions fail both women and men.

By approaching genre in this way, Conrad's fiction also poses broader
questions about the confining nature of popular representations and
their broader effect on cultural norms. If *The Secret Agent* is compelling in part because it is "Winnie Verloc's story" it is not just because he
has shown the effects of politics in the life of an individual like Winnie,
a woman alone (Conrad 1924a, xv). Winnie is, in the words of the
Assistant Commissioner, "a genuine wife"—a woman who is subject, in
other words, to genuine oppression (Conrad 1924b, 222). Much more
so than readers recognized for much of the twentieth century, Conrad's
oeuvre is powerfully engaged with the conditions of women's lives and
the outrage and frustration that their experiences generate: the politics of
these late novels are the politics of gender.

References

Auden, W.H. 1948. "The Guilty Vicarage." *The Dyer's Hand and Other Essays*,
    146–158. New York: Random House.
Cohen, Paula Marantz. 1994. "The Ideological Transformation of Conrad's *The
    Secret Agent* into Hitchcock's *Sabotage*." *Literature/Film Quarterly* 22 (3):
    199–209.
Conrad, Joseph. 1924a. Author's Note to *The Secret Agent: A Simple Tale*, vii–xv.
    Garden City, NY: Doubleday, Page, and Company.
———. 1924b. *The Secret Agent: A Simple Tale*. Garden City, NY: Doubleday,
    Page, and Company.

DeKoven, Marianne. 1999. "Modernism and Gender". In *The Cambridge Companion to Modernism*, ed. Michael Levenson, 174–193. Cambridge: Cambridge University Press.

Wollaeger, Mark. 2006. *Modernism, Media, and Propaganda: British Narrative from 1900 to 1945*. Princeton: Princeton University Press.

INDEX

© The Editor(s) (if applicable) and The Author(s) 2017   163
E.B. Harrington, *Conrad's Sensational Heroines*,
DOI 10.1007/978-3-319-63297-1

H

Hampson, Robert, 3, 5, 10, 54, 83,
    93, 98, 99, 101, 104, 145, 147,
    149, 153
Hassim, in "The Rescue", 127
Hawthorn, Jeremy, 37, 38, 46, 48, 67
Heart of Darkness (Conrad), 86, 118,
    137n1. *See also* Marlow
    critique of, 2, 4, 10, 27, 32, 43,
        45, 48, 56, 64, 70, 78, 79, 88,
        103, 114, 115, 134
Heroic male rescuer, captain as, 2, 134
Hervey, Alvan
    departure of, 118, 119
    description of, 113
    male dominance of, 109, 111
    narcissism of, 116
    perceived brutality of, 113
    privileged culture of, 110
    superficiality of, 113, 114
    understanding of, 117, 118
Hervey, Mrs.
    departure of, 114, 118
    discontent of, 109, 120
    honesty of, 113, 116, 129
    individuality of, 109, 115, 116, 119
    infidelity of, 118
    marriage of, 108, 120
    sexual liberation of, 115
Heyst, Axel
    departure of, 11, 85
    in *Victory*, 3, 7, 55, 84, 99, 104, 156
    Lena and, 54, 82, 86
    struggles of, 81
    upbringing of, 60, 80
Hitchcock, Alfred, 155, 156, 158, 159
Honesty, of Hervey, Mrs., 113, 116, 129
Hunter, Allan, 7, 19
Hypocrisy, in "A Smile of Fortune",
    7, 139
Hysteria, insanity, and mental disease,
    in women, 3, 135

I

"The Idiots" (Conrad), 10, 17–24,
    27–28, 95–96. *See also* Bacadou,
    Jean-Pierre; Bacadou, Susan
    Chance relating to, 10, 12, 59, 61,
        62, 71
    degenerative behavior in, 11, 17, 20
    family tragedy in, 17
    female protagonist in, 17
    grandmother in, 24
    inheritance in, 18
    mariticidal murder in, 17
    maternal passion in, 8, 11, 23, 42
    mentally disadvantaged children in,
        18, 62
    mother's death in, 134
    parental and spousal roles in, 18
Illegitimate son, of Jacobus, E., 6, 138
Immada, in "The Rescue", 124, 127
Individuality, of Hervey, Mrs., 115,
    119
Infidelity
    of Hervey, Mrs., 118
    of Travers, E., 124, 129
Intimate violence, 84
Isolation
    of Jacobus, Alice, 3, 13
    psychological trauma and, 3, 13

J

Jacobus, Alfred
    Alice as child of, 5–7, 137–139
    lack of personal character of, 5, 137
Jacobus, Alice
    abuse of, 6, 138
    as child of Alfred, 5–7, 137–139
    as embowered women, 1, 133
    atavism of, 8, 140
    captain and, 10, 142
    demeanor of, 3, 135
    fears of, 10, 142

CPSIA information can be obtained
at www.ICGtesting.com
Printed in the USA
LVHW030851261119
638462LV00012B/1236/P